Misophonia Matters

An Advocacy-Based Approach to Coping with
Misophonia for Adults and Clinicians

by Shaylynn Hayes-Raymond

MISOPHONIA MATTERS © 2024

Published by Misophonia International
Columbia, Missouri

Distributed by Imperceptions Press

Cover art and print/eBook design
by Imperceptions Press

Edited by Harrison Porter

Don't want no penthouse,
bathtub, streetcars, taxis

Noise in my ear

So no matter how they
coax him

I'll stay right here

- *Civilization*
(Bongo, Bongo, Bongo)
The Andrews Sisters

Contents

Dedication

Thank you to Jennifer Jo Brout for our work together as advocates and for everything you taught me about misophonia.

Thank you to Susan Nesbit for allowing me to use her sensory diet and explanation of Sensory Integration and Sensory Processing Disorder as part of this book.

Thank you to my husband Preston Raymond and my mother and father Michelle and Roderick Hayes for all your support and understanding of misophonia—I know this is not easy for you.

Introduction

At nineteen years old, I lost my ability to fully take part in the world around me. Unlike common sensory impairments, I did not lose my ability to hear, smell, or see. Instead, I suffer from a condition that amplifies each of these. When I touch, when I look, I am feeling everything around me—and it does not feel pleasant. Imagine you are trapped with the same sound for hours. A slow torture will begin to encapsulate your body. For sufferers of misophonia, a strange yet real condition, this torture is immediate. From the drop of a fork, or the slight pitch of a whistle, we are derailed.

Those that have not heard of misophonia are often surprised by the condition. Some are perplexed by its nature and have trouble believing that it is more than an annoyance.

For sufferers of misophonia, we are confronted with an immediate fight/flight response to otherwise normal sounds and visuals.

When I first discovered my condition, I went through many emotions. The first was relief that I was not crazy. This was quickly followed by dismay. While I did have a name for the disorder, there was no cure. Soon, my dismay turned to frustration. Information on my disorder, when available, was often wrong or even blatantly manipulative. Charlatans were capitalizing off Google, Wikipedia, and the editors at sites as big as WebMD were not paying attention to scientists. I spent the first year of this disorder wondering what would come of everything—if there was no cure and no one was paying attention, I did not know how I was supposed to keep going.

Advocating for an unknown condition is multifaceted. For some, my story has become a beacon, and my efforts are a force to be reckoned with. To many, I have become a symbol of hope. I often feel shame when I sit in my worst moments, void of promise and inspiration. While others look up to me, I spend many moments lost in my own dreariness. The truth is that I am uncomfortable with any idolization for my actions. I am an advocate not for notoriety, but for the ultimate end goal. I am an advocate because I hope for a world in which people like me can walk freely on the streets or have dinner in a restaurant.

While stigma is still a problem for many disorders, I have never had as hard of a time as I do with my disorder that is completely unknown. If I must explain my ADHD, Anxiety, or Depression to others, I can point them to research studies—to evidence and proof that these disorders are real. For misophonia, these studies are happening, but at a slow pace, and while there is no treatment, research has accumulated in the last six years.

I do not mind being an advocate for my disorder. It is invigorating to know that my day-to-day work may have an impact on my own life and that of current and future sufferers. However, that does not mean I am not tired. I am tired of typing and saying the same sentences over and over. I am tired of having to justify my disorder whenever I meet a new person. I am tired of explaining why I cannot go to restaurants, or why jingling keys, tapping hands, or whistling turn me into a nightmare—crying and all.

When I first discovered what "misophonia" was, I had an entirely different story to tell. I was relieved there was a name. I was also scared that I had a disorder that seemed to be under-researched and would be at risk of being stigmatized.

Most people that I have talked to with misophonia have been suffering since they were children. However, I am one of the late bloomers. Regardless of when it came to be, misophonia is an extremely isolating disorder. I was 16 when I showed my first symptoms, but they were not strong. It was not until 19 when the full force of misophonia hit me like a freight train. Since then, I have felt its wrath clasp around my throat, taking over several aspects of my life. My first blog post on misophonia was written before I even knew there was a name—before I had anything to go on. I remember writing in frustration, tears not far off, as I wondered why I was so messed up? Why, all of a sudden, I was having so much trouble with sights and sounds? When I first came across misophonia, I described it as ruining my life. I did not understand why, but these everyday movements and sounds were turning normal situations into a terrible prison.

I attributed my first triggers to an anxiety disorder as well as major depressive disorder. Small movements or rocking back and forth were enough to cause near panic attacks. If a desk was not sitting on the floor properly, I would lose it. If a classmate was making loud, distracting noises, I would complain to the teacher. It did not always get me far, but if they did not help, I would leave. I was not the most attentive student in high school.

On January 27th of 2014, I wrote a blog post expressing my confusion and rage regarding what I now know as misophonia. Please bear in mind that this was written before I had any idea about misophonia. The title was "I Do Not Know What To Do." Below, it is recopied in full.

When I first came to university, I did not remember why I had been so distracted and annoyed in high school. Homework is not hard; the reading is fine. What I cannot deal with is the burden that my anxiety can be in a classroom environment. Half of the time I have a scowl on my face in class and probably come off as a bit of a condescending witch. Whenever people whistle, click their pen, or shake their legs, it is extremely distracting for me and for a reason I cannot explain it sends me into a horrible state. Leg twitching in my peripheral vision has literally brought me to tears. I am so frustrated that I cannot just "get over it". I understand restless leg syndrome is a real thing but so is the anxiety that I suffer every time I enter a classroom. I understand that it would be rude to approach somebody and ask them to please stop torturing me.

Instead, I often stew and try not to get upset, but instead I usually just end up irrationally angry. Oftentimes I can actually feel the vibrations on the floor from people shaking behind me, even if they are far away. A couple of weeks ago, I started hyperventilating when somebody was whistling. Why? The sharp noise was so unbearable to me. I honestly do not know what I am supposed to do about this. Breathing exercises, telling myself it is out of my control and "thinking positive" are hopeless. I do not want to constantly glare at my friends like they are the worst thing in the world just because they are shaking their feet. I am actually sorry it bugs me this much, but I cannot stop. Sometimes I find myself sitting in my room anxious about going to class just because of my triggers. I just feel alone in this and that I must sound ridiculous to others. Aside from hiding in my room wearing ear plugs and only ever communicating via Skype, I am unsure of a fix to this.

My first "real" trigger was whistling. I would go into a rage and nearly cry whenever I was faced with it. Some people would whistle on purpose, because they did not understand the severity of my reaction. I remember being upset for hours after this would happen, and that confused me significantly. Then, one day, my mother's foot-shaking really started to bother me. Soon after, the sound of singing and country music really sent me over the edge. This caused many fights and much confusion. Why was I so intolerant? It made no sense to me.

While there are many common triggers that seem to arise in numerous people, not everybody has the same triggers. We are not all the same, so that makes it even harder to raise awareness. However, regardless of what a person is triggered by, we are still triggered, and it can be very disorienting. There is no logical reason to freak out— we can feel crazy, guilty, and downright ridiculous. It is full of fury. The simple clicking of a pen can feel like we are trapped in a cavern with a jackhammer. Melodrama aside, I believe that a good life is possible with misophonia and even more possible with the right coping skills. I am no longer afraid of misophonia, and I truly believe that there is much hope to be had!

The International Misophonia Foundation (IMF) is a project that is of great importance to me, Shaylynn Hayes-Raymond. As the co-founder of Misophonia International, and the remaining owner, I had questions about where my journey was going to lead following eight years of advocacy. I feel as though Misophonia International has provided valuable information over the past decade, and I am proud of the classes that I took part in running with Misophonia Education. Yet, I felt as though there was something more that could be achieved. As somebody who has misophonia, who has written about it, and who has dedicated all their time to the disorder, I knew there had to be something big for the next step...

Thus, The International Misophonia Foundation was formed alongside a wonderful initial board of directors. We are still in the process of beginning, but I am so happy to be on this journey. Over the past two years, I have been working on a counselling degree, and as I near the finish line on that project, I am happy that my work starting this nonprofit is going to coincide with clinical interests in misophonia. I know that there is a long road ahead, but I am excited for what is to come.

A main reason for my interest in creating the IMF is to have an organization that is conducting research and surveying the people who actually have misophonia. All too often, researchers do their initial research and forget to ask those who have the disorder. My goal for the IMF is to put people and families of those with misophonia ahead of all other goals—whether that is academic or clinical, we the people with misophonia should be front and center in alleviating our own suffering.

Part 1: Psychoeducation

What is Misophonia?

"What is Misophonia?" is one of the most contentious questions that I have ever dealt with. If you ask some, it is a psychiatric condition where people are overreacting to stimuli. I do not believe this. For me, misophonia is atypical neurological processing of audial and visual information (Kumar et al., 2017). However, it remains a contentious question. The disorder continues to make people's lives worse, and yet we cannot land on a definition of what it is exactly.

To me, misophonia is the worst thing that has ever happened to me. Misophonia is a condition which means that every part of my life is now a negotiation. From a purely emotional and life-based perspective, misophonia is a constant flux of negotiating triggers and the possibility of triggers. No amount of scientific debate takes away the fact that misophonia is something that causes great suffering and pain to those who have it.

Scientifically, I believe that misophonia is a neurophysiological disorder where otherwise non-aversive stimuli cause a fight-flight-freeze reaction (Brout et al., 2018), yet that does not say very much when it comes to the everyday lives of those with misophonia. As scientists argue in academic articles about *what part of the brain* is impacted by misophonia and as they do treatment studies which turn out to have essentially placebo levels of treatment (and yet tote them as "helpful"), we are still here with this condition wondering… what exactly this condition is that is akin to our own personal hell.

Research and understanding of misophonia are new in the grand scheme of neuroscience and psychology. The term misophonia was first coined in 2001 when audiologists Drs. Jastreboff and Jastreboff discovered that there was a differentiation in their practice between tinnitus, hyperacusis, and misophonia patients (Jastreboff and Jastreboff, 2001). The culture surrounding misophonia is one of online support groups and websites which band together to help researchers understand their condition and share their commonalities to fill in the gaps of a literature that has yet to fully conceptualize or honor their experiences. Some of these communities include the use of social media communities, internet websites, or nonprofits which advocate for sufferers with the disorder. Misophonia sufferers often consider themselves "misophones" in their communities, and they are very vocal about research and stigma surrounding their disorder (Misophonia International, n.d.). Persons with misophonia are often upset by the prospect of exposure therapy, and feel that if exposure worked, they would all be cured as there is no way to fully limit exposure to otherwise normal sensory stimuli such as coughing, chewing, whistling, and pen tapping.

Although misophonia is in its infancy as a recognized disorder, it has been shown to be "associated with altered brain activity in the auditory cortex and salience network" (Schröder et al., 2019), as well as having a brain basis including the sensory motor system (Kumar et al., 2017; 2021). Research has found that the amount of exposure does not change the emotional response to misophonia and thus exposure therapy would not be an effective form of treatment (Rosenthal et al., 2022). One study showed that persons with misophonia share similar traits to those with autism (Rinaldi et al., 2023), further justifying the use of a sensory regulation-based approach to misophonia. Accommodations for misophonia have also been shown to be beneficial in a school environment, and thus could be similarly useful in a workplace environment (Porcaro et al., 2019). There have been some statistical findings suggesting that CBT can be helpful for misophonia (Jager et al., 2021); however, the community's perceptions of CBT and differentiating between types of CBT are important when moving forward with any client. For example, some CBT helps people to change their beliefs about a trigger and learn to live in a world with that trigger, whereas other practitioners might try exposure therapy and there is no one size fits all for CBT. It is important when treating and conceptualizing misophonia to remember how "To date, no randomized controlled trials evaluating treatments for misophonia have been published" (Brout et al., 2018).

What is Sensory Processing Disorder?

By Susan Nesbit, M.S., OT.

In the 1960s, Dr. Ayres described Sensory Integration Dysfunction (SID), including tactile defensiveness (Ayres, 1968; 1972; 1979). She suggested that children who overreact to touch (e.g., they do not like getting their hair and nails cut, will not wear certain textures of clothes, and avoid activities such as finger painting) have a protective tactile system that is always on. The discriminative tactile system (e.g., knowing that you are feeling your keys in the bottom of your purse without looking at them) is not overriding the protective tactile system, and the unimportant tactile information does not get filtered out. With the bombardment of protective tactile information, a child with tactile defensiveness is in a pattern of fight-or-flight (e.g., they are unable to sit still and feel the keys in their hands). Dr. Ayres further proposed that activities with deep pressure (e.g., hugging and jumping) enable the discriminative tactile system to override the protective tactile system so the unimportant tactile information can be filtered out and the child can be available for learning.

Imagine a child with tactile defensiveness playing on a seesaw. The seat with the protective tactile system (sympathetic nervous system) stays up, causing the child to flail (to wildly swing their arms and legs) with anger and other negative emotions. The seat with the discriminative tactile system (parasympathetic nervous system) does not go up, so the child is unable to enjoy the seesaw. Children need to balance the seesaw by alternating the seat for the protective tactile system going up (so they can run if they see a fire) with the seat for the discriminative tactile system going up (so they can sit still without flailing, and they can have fun and learn in a safe environment).

In the 1980s, other scholars proposed that defensiveness exists in other sensory channels, and several other types of sensory defensiveness were labeled and described, including auditory (sounds), visual (sights), and olfactory (smell). Because the protective and the discriminative tactile systems address only tactile defensiveness, and not defensiveness in the other sensory channels, the more recent scholars theorized that the amygdala is the filter, with the inhibitory fibers not overriding the excitatory fibers. The excitatory fibers are constantly firing, thereby letting in unimportant information so a person is wired for fight, flight, or freeze. The sympathetic and the parasympathetic nervous systems are unbalanced. These scholars suggested using activities that provide deep pressure and slow linear movement to help the inhibitory fibers override the excitatory fibers.

Moving into the twenty-first century, Dr. Lucy Jane Miller coined the terminology commonly used today. Sensory Integration Disorder is now referred to as a Sensory Processing Disorder (SPD) (Miller et al., 2009; 2021), which is an umbrella term with three primary diagnostic categories: (a) Sensory Modulation Disorder (SMD), (b) Sensory Discrimination Disorder (SDD), and Sensory-Based Motor Disorder (SBMD). Each diagnostic category has subtypes.

SMD has three subtypes: (a) Sensory Over-Responsivity (SOR), (b) Sensory Under-Responsivity (SUR), and Sensory Craving (SC). Persons can have SOR, SUR, and/or SC in one or more of the various sensory channels. Sensory channels include the following: auditory (sounds), visual (sights), tactile (touch), pain (physical distress), olfactory (smells), gustatory (tastes), proprioception/vestibular (position/movement), air temperature (hot or cold), and interoception (e.g., hunger pangs). Persons with SOR perceive the input from one or more of the sensory channels as noxious, harmful, or threatening. For example, a child with an auditory over-responsivity might cover their ears when someone whistles or jangles their keys. In contrast, persons with SUR barely perceive the input from one or more of the sensory channels. For example, a child with bumps and bruises might feel minimal pain. And a person with SC seeks input from one or more of the sensory channels. Examples include a child touching and/or smelling objects as they walk through a room, a child who seeks movement having difficulty sitting still, and a child who seeks proprioceptive input (pressure) intentionally bumping into things, including people.

SDD has six subtypes: (a) Auditory, (b) Visual, (c) Tactile, (d) Taste/Smell, (e) Position/Movement, and (f) Interoception.

SBMD has two subtypes: Dyspraxia and Postural Disorder. Persons with dyspraxia (poor motor planning) have problems doing new or unfamiliar tasks such as learning to tie shoelaces. They do not learn to tie their shoelaces automatically (without thinking), and when they feel stressed, the task of tying is even more challenging. Postural disorders include poor balance and low muscle tone.

Misophonia and auditory over-responsivity might overlap. (Note: SPD is used interchangeably with the term auditory over-responsivity. To be in sync with others, I will use the term SPD when referring to a sensory modulation disorder, including auditory over-responsivity.)

Misophonia is a strong dislike or hatred of specific sounds. Persons with misophonia dislike soft or loud repetitive sounds, especially sounds made by the mouth. Triggers include chomping food, slurping a drink, snapping gum, humming, and whistling. Other triggers include opening a bag of chips, cracking knuckles, and texting with the volume on. Sounds are not triggers when the person with misophonia makes them. Sounds are triggers when another person makes them.

When exposed to a trigger, people with misophonia feel anger, disgust, and hate. In contrast, people with hyperacusis feel pain from loud and/or high-pitched sounds such as sirens and alarms, screeching brakes on subways or buses, silverware clanking against dishes, children's screams, and clapping. Some loud repetitive triggers overlap with the triggers for misophonia. For example, silverware clanking against dishes is listed as a trigger for each condition.

People with SPD dislike all of the above sounds. The emotional manifestations (anger, disgust, and hate) and the behaviors (fight, flight, or freeze) of persons with misophonia and SPD seem similar.

Some persons diagnosed with misophonia are reported to have visual sensitivities in addition to their auditory sensitivities. The term misokinesia has been used to mean a hatred of movement. People with misokinesia strongly dislike seeing movements such as someone twirling their hair around and around their finger, someone moving their legs up and down while sitting, and someone chewing food or gum with their open mouth.

Persons with SPD typically have problems in more than one sensory channel; therefore, over-responsiveness to inputs such as visual and tactile in addition to auditory over-responsivity suggest SPD. However, the auditory sensory channel might be the only sense affected in SPD. Therefore, the question of whether misophonia and SPD are linked needs to be investigated. Please bear in mind that the current lack of research does not rule out a potential link between these two conditions.

SPD is thought to be a neurodevelopmental condition, meaning that it is a disorder within the brain that affects emotions, self-control, attention/memory, and learning throughout the lifespan. Research is ongoing; however, the neurobiological mechanisms and the implicated structures in the brain are poorly documented. The etiologies (causes) are unknown, but a genetic vulnerability is possible in some persons with SPD. Fewer studies exist for misophonia. Whether this condition is neurological or learned from experiences is controversial. Research is needed to investigate the similarities and the differences between SPD and misophonia and to investigate the possible co-occurrence of these conditions.

The potential exists that some persons have been misdiagnosed, and an incorrect diagnosis could lead to the wrong treatments, which could worsen the symptoms. The causes of misophonia and SPD could be different. Causes guide treatments; therefore, research to find the causes for misophonia and SPD is important.

Occupational therapists evaluate for SPD with informal tests, such as observations and interviews, and with formal tests that are standardized for validity and reliability. Formal tests include the Sensory Profiles and the Sensory Processing Measures. These two batteries of tests use age-appropriate and environmentally appropriate (home versus classroom) forms.

Occupational therapists have been treating children and adults diagnosed with Sensory Integration Disorder (SID), now called Sensory Processing Disorder (SPD), since the 1960s. Some people come for intervention in a sensory gym with a variety of swings, climbing structures, balls, bolsters (rolls), mats, and other equipment to provide body movement and proprioception (deep pressure). The other sensory systems are treated as well. For example, sensory bins are used for persons with tactile problems.

Occupational therapists work with students in schools, giving teachers suggestions to help students with SPD stay on task. Suggestions include providing movement by sending the student on errands such as taking the class attendance to the office and/or allowing them to sharpen pencils; providing movement while sitting by using a wobble chair or a standard chair with a wobble cushion; providing pressure against the student's torso (trunk) by allowing them to sit backwards in their chair; providing movement and pressure on different body parts by allowing the student to switch positions (e.g., alternating between a sitting position—including sitting on their legs, a standing position, and stomach lying on the carpet); and providing structured fidgeting by allowing the student to rub their hand(s) across Velcro taped inside the top of a desk, twist the pieces at the top of a fidget pencil, play with a fidget toy, and/or press their feet against the legs of their desk.

Occupational therapists also work with parents, giving home programs with sensory activities and making suggestions for modifying (changing) the home environment. The goals of classroom and home modifications are to reduce the number of noxious stimuli and to provide ways to stay calm or regain composure when triggered.

SPD has no cure. However, the symptoms can be temporarily lessened through a variety of treatments, including sensory diets. Similar to a diet of food, the input from a sensory diet does not last indefinitely in the body. The input lasts one to two hours, or less when stressed by noxious stimuli.

Sensory diets include activities for pressure and movement. Activities can include hiking, walking, or running; doing animal walks (e.g., elephant, bear, rabbit, frog, duck, and crab); wheelbarrow walking; floor or chair pushups; "play" wrestling; bouncing on a hopper ball (they come in adult sizes); jumping (e.g., up and down with both legs together or jumping jacks) on the floor or a mini-trampoline (use a regular trampoline if one is available); playing on a variety of swings, climbing structures, and slides; doing yoga (classes and books/flash cards are available for adults and children); using fidget toys; manipulating Play-Doh or modeling clay; and coloring mandalas (beginning at the center). Doing heavy work, including taking out the garbage, mowing the lawn, carrying the laundry, and pushing furniture to vacuum, can be included in a sensory diet.

I am a pediatric occupational therapist, and I have misophonia and SPD. To avoid becoming overwhelmed by triggers, I control my environment as much as possible. For example, I ask people not to whistle or crack their knuckles. I leave the room if someone is chomping food. I have been called controlling; however, the alternative is melting down or shutting down.

When initially triggered, I typically remain calm. I can think and be proactive. I can stay calm until the frequency (number) of the triggers increases, the intensity (strength) of just one trigger increases, and/or the duration (length of time) of just one trigger extends. When the triggers accumulate, I become overwhelmed.

When I become overwhelmed, I am unable to think and I become reactive. I have an "adult" meltdown by snapping at the person whom I view to be noxious or by crying. I try to reserve my crying until I am alone, but I am not always successful. If I do not have a meltdown, then I shut down (withdraw) and I do not listen.

I can become overwhelmed with sound triggers alone, but with the addition of other triggers—sights, smells, being hot, and/or being hungry—I more easily become overwhelmed and I have a bigger meltdown or I withdraw more deeply. I experience what I call the "additive effect", which I will describe later in a different section.

For people with SPD, and possibly with misophonia, I suggest using a sensory diet (examples given above). When I am unable to leave the negative situation to do some of the activities such as walking, I hug myself by squeezing my torso with my arms crossed, and I cross my legs at my knees and my ankles (I am flexible). Sometimes I clasp my hands together and squeeze—under the table when possible—I try to be inconspicuous. (Note: I have successfully explained to social workers and psychologists who work with persons with SPD that by crossing my arms around my body and by crossing my legs, I am not communicating that I am closed to them and not listening. Instead, through the pressure provided in these positions, I can remain calm to listen.)

I also try to reframe my negative thoughts by thinking about something positive, e.g., this meeting will be over in 15 minutes and then I will get a gourmet coffee. Sometimes, sounds that I enjoy mingle with sounds that I hate, and I try to focus on the sounds that I enjoy. For example, if someone is triggering me on the NYC subway, I will try to listen to the wheels moving along the tracks. Sometimes I visualize walking in a forest surrounded by the sounds that I love (e.g., a waterfall gliding over the rocks into a pond, the rustle of the pine needles under my feet, and the singing birds perched in the trees). I visualize watching the white fluffy clouds moving across the cerulean-blue sky. I stop to smell the roses. I feel the rain on my skin. Sometimes I breathe deeply, counting as I inhale and exhale. Sometimes I progressively relax my muscles. But when I am tipped over the edge and I cannot think, visualizing the triggering person getting run over by a tractor-trailer truck is helpful. (Note: reframing, mindfulness, visualization, deep breathing, and progressive muscle relaxation work for me only when the triggers are few, not intense, and not lasting a long time.)

Sensory information accumulates. Imagine a set of triggers: You are at a low level of arousal and your alarm clock rings. You push the snooze button and it goes off again in only 5 minutes and you are still tired. You get out of bed and step on a toy. You go to make coffee and discover that you have no cream. You pick up the cereal box and it opens on the bottom, spilling onto the floor. Your child will not get dressed. You finally leave the house and back your car out of your garage, hitting your child's bicycle. By now, even a person without misophonia or SPD might be on a high level of arousal (sensory overload). Before driving your car, try to take a break to reset your level of arousal from high to normal.

To describe what I call the additive effect, I will use my auditory and visual triggers in a mathematical equation. I will give a score of 2 (for mathematical purposes only; I am not using a scale to rate how much I hate the trigger) to hearing someone chomping their food. And I will give a score of 2 for seeing that person chewing with their mouth open. In this scenario, 2 + 2 does not equal 4. Instead, 2 + 2 equals 5.

When possible, modify your environment to reduce the frequency (number), the intensity (strength), and the duration (length of time) of the triggers. Modifying the environment is helpful for persons with misophonia and/or SPD.

For people with SPD, I gave examples of activities for a sensory diet in an earlier section. Identify the sensory activities that work best for you. Do a sensory diet for 5-10 minutes. Because the sensory activities are part of a diet, you may need to do them every one or two hours. You may need to do them more often if triggered. Another easy-to-do technique is self-hugging, as described in an earlier question.

Bear in mind that if the cause of misophonia is different than the cause of SPD, then a sensory diet may not be effective for misophonia. Some scholars speculate, however, that misophonia also could be neurologically based, and perhaps the same structures in the central nervous system (the brain) are involved.

If you live with a person with misophonia or SPD, I suggest allowing that person to have control, or at least perceived control, to create a structured and supportive environment. By perceived control, I mean giving choices;

however, every choice is acceptable to you. In an example: You need to do two errands and take your child along. You know that they dislike hearing noises in stores. You can give them the choice of which store they would like to go to first. You can say, "I know you hate shopping (empathy); however, we need to shop for dinner and buy daddy a new hammer. Which store would you like to go to first? The grocery store or the hardware store?" You are setting limits with two acceptable choices. You also can solve problems together by asking them how they can cope (be less angry) with the noise. Bear in mind that persons with misophonia and SPD are controlling in an effort to reduce triggers (noxious stimuli) to prevent sensory overload.

Our Voices and Needs

The entire concept of *Misophonia Matters* is drawn from the idea that no one understands misophonia more than the people who have misophonia. Whether you are reading this as a sufferer of misophonia, or a clinician who is working with those with misophonia, the important takeaway is that misophonia is a complex condition that is poorly understood.

Although it was nearly a decade ago, I remember like it was yesterday hearing Kathie Lee and Hoda speak about misophonia in a segment. The two talked about the term misophonia, mentioned chewing rage, and then gawked about how the disorder did not sound real—and even called it "misophoney". Dr. Phil berated a person with misophonia on his show. The press has dubbed misophonia chewing rage and treated sufferers like circus clowns, an amusing population they had never heard of before, ripe for berating. With its status as a lesser-known disorder, many have not yet got the message that mocking persons with misophonia is cruel.

This stigmatization makes it harder for sufferers of the disorder to feel safe explaining their condition to loved ones, employers, school staff, and other important individuals in their lives. Stigma is more than something we internalize, it shapes the way one interacts with the world, and can impact the level of support and understanding that an individual receives. Numerous misophonia sufferers have exclaimed to me upon learning that there is a name for the disorder, "Oh my god, I thought I was just crazy!" This pervasive view that sufferers of misophonia are strange, crazy, or overreacting is one that I hope shifts through advocacy and public awareness.

The State of Misophonia Research

Misophonia research is something that I have found perplexing in my years of advocacy. As a person who does believe in the scientific process, I understand why theories need to be proven and disproven. What I do not understand is why researchers are constantly ignoring the information that has been presented to them by sufferers of the very disorder they are researching.

As more and more studies start to come out on misophonia, I am finding it hard to understand why some of these studies exist. For example, some studies have questioned whether or not *misophonia should be accommodated*, or whether or not misophonia is something that is psychiatric, or whether or not misophonia should be treated with exposure therapy or behavioral interventions. This is all despite years of sufferers of misophonia speaking out about how their therapists and clinicians have *already been trying these treatments* to no avail, and in some cases, causing more distress than before "treatment".

Of course, we need studies on *why* things do not work. After all, I cannot cite to you *why* exposure therapy for misophonia is cruel and unhelpful, yet at this point I think it is important that we do not ignore the perceptions of people with misophonia who have already been treated by therapists with exposure therapy. If these forms of therapy worked, do you not think that *somebody* would have said so? There are hundreds of thousands of people with misophonia on the internet, yet you would be hard-pressed to find a support group that supports the concept of exposure therapy. Are these voices not important to the design of a study for misophonia?

Much of this was the ethos of starting The International Misophonia Foundation, a non-profit registered in Missouri dedicated to misophonia and sensory processing disorders. If those who have misophonia are not included in the design of research, then the research might never reflect our actual values and experiences. It is one thing to collect data from individuals with misophonia and come to conclusions. It is another thing entirely for the design of the research to always have the community in mind.

I recently had a conversation with a notable researcher in the misophonia community who responded to a petition in favor of misophonia accommodations by telling me that accommodations are "counterproductive, hinders effective treatment, and if it is at the high level it prevents success".

To me this is a strange claim since we do not have an effective treatment for misophonia to hinder. How do you hinder something that has yet to actually exist? I am also unsure what level of success could be stopped by accommodations, particularly since most people with misophonia simply want to live their lives without feeling grueling torture.

If researchers are worried that overaccommodating will lead to unrealistic expectations of the world, I think that is fair, but I counter the point by saying that alleviating your suffering in some aspects of your life can make your quality of life better overall, and then your nervous system is less taxed and more able to handle the bad situations as they come.

The opposite of accommodations would be to desensitize to the sounds. If this worked, I think all of us would be cured because most triggers for misophonia are ever-present. This is not some phobia where we can avoid the stimuli and live our lives sheltered from fear. Everyday sounds (and visuals) are causing us great distress, and the longer our nervous systems are taxed, the worse we feel. For example, after a long day of being triggered I will simply shut down and no longer be able to think properly or respond. I practically feel catatonic, and then I get a migraine and feel sick.

We also need to stop ignoring decades of sensory processing disorder research that talks about using interoception and proprioception to lower arousal, rather than simply looking for random solutions where they do not need to exist. The willful blindness of researchers to ignore over 40 years of relevant research is frustrating, to say the least. Auditory over responsivity was not a new phenomenon before being carelessly named misophonia in 2001, but now we are doing new research without any heading, completely disregarding the work of Jean Ayres, Lucy Miller, Teresa May Benson, and other sensory researchers. Let us stop pretending that there is no research to look at and actually start talking to other researchers. Everybody wants to be the one to "cure" misophonia, and in the meantime, they are making suggestions that actively harm our communities. Enough is enough.

An effective treatment for misophonia does not exist. If we knew about it, then we would gladly share it. Therefore, what treatments are accommodations making less effective? I am unsure how it could, since the disorder is in a preliminary stage of investigation. Yet, what we do know is that the quality of life of these very real people is made better by making adjustments to their environment. All these researchers are doing is adding more shame and stigma to an already misunderstood phenomenon. We are struggling enough... let me keep my headphones, my earplugs, and my ability to leave the room!

Since misophonia is a newly described disorder, and one for which a consensus is still being reached, there is much room for researchers to get things wrong. In fact, getting things wrong is often an important part of the scientific approach. This is why replication is one of the most important things in studies—if something cannot be replicated, it is not yet seen as truth. And yet, despite this, charlatans are often quick to tote "studies" (often singular case studies without replication) as "proof" that their treatment or theory is legitimate. This is dangerous.

I want to first point out that technically speaking, anybody can be published as a researcher. Traditional barriers of entry like having a research center or university backing are becoming less and less important with the birth of entirely online journals. More chillingly, there is a growing number of *pay to play* publications that essentially take the money of the author—go through an expedited "peer review" process—and then churn out whatever "research" was submitted under the guise of science. There is no money in rejecting numerous papers. This is why people who do not have graduate degrees or even clinical backgrounds can get into so many journals. Whether a person is a nurse, a doctor, or a journalist, their "research" can join the world with little to no barriers. Except, of course, a little money.

To further this unethical practice, the internet has little to no rules for claims and name ownership. One can be an "institute" or a "center" without ever having a physical address or license to back this claim. After all, anybody can buy a domain name with a tricky keyword and try to tell the world they are an expert. This is a frustrating reality, but one we have to live with and learn to parse and avoid for ourselves.

Even more insidious than pay to play researchers are doctorate level researchers without sufficient neuroscience background insisting that misophonia is cognitive. This is particularly pervasive with CBT research, despite little to no replicable evidence that exposure therapy or CBT is helpful for misophonia. In fact, most people with misophonia who tried exposure techniques have come back saying it was a "torturous" experience. With that said, these cognitive researchers are so shut off and set in their ways that they refuse to acknowledge research from neuroscientists like Sukhbinder Kumar (2017; 2021) which shows an entirely different picture of misophonia—and one that has been verified with brain scans, not just with case studies and conjecture.

It is very unfortunate that even at the doctorate level we have researchers who are ignoring emerging studies and toting their own irresponsible theories as scientific evidence. Even more insidious, these researchers have easier access to publication and are well-respected by their peers. I am horrified by the possibility that cognitive behavioral therapy (CBT), and more concerningly exposure therapy, will become the go-to approach for therapists worldwide merely because of half-baked research that presents misophonia as receptive to exposure—despite little evidence that it is cognitive instead of neurological.

This is flabbergasting to me. I was always taught that science is the pursuit of following the evidence, but instead, many camps of theories are emerging that are blatantly ignoring the reality, data, and brain scans of people who actually have misophonia and were studied.

Parents and sufferers must be proactive about misophonia advocacy. It is an unfortunate reality that we must be vigilant when we read "scientific" studies, but like science itself, questioning everything and seeing if there are replicated results (multiple sources) is the only way forward.

Almost every researcher on the planet would like to stand up and say that they care more about research than they do about their own ego and their own perspective on their research. I would argue that every single one of them, even the most noble and most ethical among them, is wrong. Ego is central to human experience. We appreciate our work because we believe in it, and when you spend years, and often decades, in a field, you are bound to have grown emotionally attached to your work. This becomes a problem when egos get in the way of new research, but more insidiously, of researchers who omit other studies and researchers because by speaking of their peers more often, their peers gain greater recognition.

Grants and funding are central in the research world. Notoriety and publishing credits all go toward your ability to generate funds. With this in mind, a researcher may be cautious at reaching out to a fellow expert. If that expert has *more papers than them* on a subject, this further bolsters the image of their competition. In a perfect world, there would be no competition, only good ideas, and experts working together to further the research and understanding of misophonia. And yet, we do not live in a perfect world, and probably never will.

What can be done about this? It is important that researchers are aware of other studies and are not omitting citations or perspectives on their work that paint a fuller picture of disorders, and yet, we know this happens every day across all scientific disciplines. In some cases, this may not even be professional self-interest, but a more stringent view which does not allow for reflection on cross-disciplinary studies. I am looking at you, behaviorally focused or cognitively focused groups. I am also not attacking one particular researcher. It is a grueling endeavor to finish a bachelor's degree, then a master's degree, and then an additional five or so years of doctoral study only to have to fight tooth and nail for a scrap of funding for your studies. At this point, I am sure that only gluttons for punishment are researchers because the field is so unkind and unforgiving to its dedicated members.

I think many of the problems lie with how research is funded at a policy level. Who is funding the research? Are they looking at the substantive picture of the researchers? Or is funding based on some sort of popularity contest?

Guidelines for funding research are spotty at best, and at worst they are a popularity contest. A commitment to scientific study must come from both the funders and the researchers, as well as the community that is impacted by this research. This commitment is one that must be ongoing.

As scientists go around telling the world that the "treatment" for misophonia is cognitive behavioral therapy, I think it is important to note that any findings on CBT that have been seen are akin to that of a coping skill— they help deal with the emotional after-effects of misophonia, not the misophonic moment, and certainly not as a preventative measure. You cannot CBT the misophonia away, and you surely should not be out there referring to CBT as a "treatment" for misophonia. This is a disingenuous move by researchers, clinicians, and those involved in the use of CBT to skew public perception on CBT.

I am not saying that CBT is unhelpful for misophonia. Like all coping skills approaches, there is room for CBT when we are trying to help people with misophonia mitigate the after-effects of the disorder and learn how to live in a world that is not accommodating to their sensory needs. Yet, this does not mean that CBT is the gold standard, and it absolutely does not mean that we should be toting things like exposure therapy. I repeat: if exposure worked, we would all be cured, as none of us can completely ignore stimuli. Misophonia is also not a behavioral disorder. We do not *learn* to hate sounds and we cannot *learn not to*. In fact, saying that misophonia is "hatred of sounds" in general is untrue because there is already proof that there is a brain basis and the amygdala and fight-flight response are involved (Kumar et al., 2017; 2021).

I understand that scientists are using familiar language, but they should be cautious when explaining any cognitive-based, or even sensory-based, skill for misophonia as a "treatment". The very word treatment assumes that misophonia can be mitigated by the skills learned, and that is simply not true. CBT is helpful to take the edge off and learn how to understand misophonia through worksheets and psychoeducation, but that does not mean that it should be referred to as a treatment. In fact, I would wager that calling anything a treatment at this point in time is nothing more than wishful thinking.

Much of the problem, I assume, is the reliance on "treatments" in American medicine and "psychiatric care". The use of insurance codes means that specific interventions must be referred to as treatments in order to be approved for use and reimbursement. Frankly, this entire practice is backwards and wrong, and this is why in places like Canada where I live this is unheard of and it only muddies the waters when it comes to the expectations of those receiving these "treatments". Instead, practitioners and researchers should be honest and explain CBT for what it is, a coping skill for the disorder, and not the gold standard approach to helping sufferers.

Treating Misophonia

Developing a treatment for misophonia is not an easy feat. We are in a place where clinicians and researchers are in an arms race trying to be the first to create an effective treatment for the disorder, sufferer perspectives be damned. It is my opinion that this onslaught of clinical perspectives has come oftentimes from a place of egotistical behavior rather than an earnest attempt to help sufferers of misophonia.

One of my goals for helping found The International Misophonia Foundation was to create a space for misophonia research that puts persons with misophonia and their loved ones at the forefront of misophonia research. As a person with misophonia, I have had strong reactions to some of the attempts to pathologize and treat misophonia. Oftentimes, these theories and treatment concepts are merely thrown out into the wild by practitioners who are using their own ethos and perspective, rather than asking people with misophonia what *they* think should be done for misophonia. Of course, there is always a degree where scientific rigor and expertise cannot be garnered from lay-people, but ignoring the community entirely is in my opinion both unethical and dangerous.

One such questionable study I can think about was a preprint from academics at Baylor University who said that people with misophonia should not be accommodated—even more chilling was that the people involved in this study were *children*. After a petition which I helmed circulated the internet and was delivered to Baylor, they seemingly relented on this issue. And yet, I am left wondering why we had to have this petition in the first place. I said the following to a misophonia researcher regarding academics who ignore sufferers and go on to formulate studies, shoehorn their ideas, and then blindly publish results:

> *"The issue here is that researchers are standing in their ivory towers making observations without actually diving deeper into the lives of people actually struggling from this disorder."*

I stand by these words today as strongly as the day I feverously typed them into a strongly worded email. As a person with misophonia, if a study truly showed some groundbreaking treatment, I would be jumping for joy. I would then probably cry a bunch because the level of relief that I would feel would be insurmountable. I have yet to have a moment like this when it comes to the sparce—yet growing—body of misophonia literature.

Numerous questions on misophonia have yet to be answered, let alone how to "treat" this disorder. The first question I will propose is what are we even *looking for* in a treatment? I will say that any amount of change that leads to sufferers of misophonia being better equipped to live their lives with this condition is something that should be celebrated. Yet, these small changes should not be championed as a be all and end all, especially when many people do not have access to practitioners and cannot afford the "treatments" being touted in the first place.

As a counsellor, I know that there can be meaningful changes from psychoeducation, sensory-regulation, or cognitive skills for misophonia. Yet, these changes are not a cure, but rather they are a means of living with the condition. This is something powerful and important, but it should not be overstated, lest sufferers of misophonia expect a level of change that is unrealistic and impossible based on a neurophysiological condition that may or may not see a physiological treatment any time soon.

It is my hope that this book tempers expectations whilst offering an advocacy-based approach to empowering people with misophonia and their loved ones. This is not to say that no change is possible, but merely to understand the word "treatment" from a realistic perspective. Instead, we are measuring change in ability to cope on a day-to-day basis, and not as a remediation of all symptoms entirely.

A point that I would like to make on treatment, while about a psychological condition, is that recent research has shown that antidepressants (SSRIs) may not be an effective treatment, despite many believing for years that antidepressants were a gold standard of care. This statement from recent research goes as follows: "Patients should be informed that there is no evidence that antidepressants work by correcting a chemical imbalance" (Moncrieff, 2018). My goal here is not to take a stab at antidepressants, or even to argue their efficacy as that is a scientific endeavor suited for its own publication, but to point out that we are forever learning about effective treatments for conditions that have been known for eons— let alone new ones such as misophonia.

Therefore, how then do we propose a "treatment plan" for misophonia based on advocacy if there is not enough evidence to formulate a strong opinion on the origins of the condition? The answer is by listening to people with misophonia, reviewing what we do know scientifically, and allowing the peer review process to continually review surveys and studies based on testing these proposed treatments for misophonia. The goal of this approach is not to fit misophonia into any particular practitioner's mold, but to ask those with misophonia *what they are feeling* and *what made them feel better*, whilst providing an advocacy-based framework and coping skills that show a measurable positive change for those with misophonia.

There is no faster way to get me to cringe than to declare yourself an "expert" on misophonia. While I understand that expertise is something we often strive for in many topics, a newly researched disorder like misophonia is not the place to say you are an expert. How can one be an expert on a topic that has not even yet been declared a disorder by bodies such as the American Psychiatric Association or the International Classification of Diseases (ICD)?

If one presents their position on misophonia from an expert approach, this can be disastrous for sufferers of misophonia if the approach used by the practitioner has little to no effect on their misophonia. Could you imagine seeing a practitioner for anxiety who is proclaimed as an expert, and then coming out of several sessions with little to no impact on your anxiety? Surely this experience would be hard to live with! It is also rather egotistical to declare yourself an expert on any neurophysiological or psychological disorder.

What is the Misophonia Matters Approach?

The Misophonia Matters approach is an approach that I developed that puts advocacy at the forefront of conceptualizing misophonia. Misophonia Matters is designed to be a flexible approach that puts self-advocacy center stage, rather than only looking at misophonia from one therapeutic lens. Instead, the clinicians who are working with misophonia sufferers pick and choose interventions based on their client's needs, all while realizing that misophonia is a condition that must be accommodated and navigated in a world that does not meet the needs of the person with misophonia. For example, no amount of cognitive behavioral therapy will change the fact that somebody whistling elicits a fight-flight-freeze response in the sufferer of misophonia, so requisite negotiations and world navigations are necessary for improving the quality of life of a person with misophonia.

This misophonia coping plan is based on psychoeducation mixed with sensory regulation and cognitive and psychological skills. The following outlines what the Misophonia Matters approach is, and how it can be implemented practically either through self-help or with a clinician.

The Misophonia Matters Course of Action

A. The use of an assessment tool for misophonia such as the Duke Misophonia Questionnaire to determine clinical implications of misophonia and level of impairment.

B. Psychoeducation resources and education for either the family or for the individual. This psychoeducation must include an explanation of the expected change and inform sufferers that they should not expect 100% mitigation of symptoms.

C. Goal-taking with the client to check in and see how they feel after learning. Guidance on the next steps of the therapy. Possible paths are likely to be followed in any order during the treatment progression but are likely to be used at some point.

D. Pathways:

    I.   Advocacy and explanations.

    II.   Accommodations and negotiations which are focused on both self (client) and therapist (accessibility plans/etc.), and which are complemented by communication skills for situations with misophonia triggers (worksheets and homework).

    III.   Sensory-based coping skills for the misophonic moment (worksheets and homework, can vary from therapist to therapist and from client to client).

    IV.   Cognitive and psychological (including narrative) approach to self-dialogue of misophonia and what this means for the world.

E. Measure seeing if there was change throughout this process such as using the Duke Misophonia Questionnaire or another measure once more.
F. Follow-up which specifically seeks sufferer perspectives and family perspectives on the experience.

At this time, the Matters Approach has not been verified through academic research and is thus a proposal. However, in the future, there are plans to test the Matters Approach through vigorous academic research. That, of course, takes time.

Section D, which highlights the types of interventions for misophonia, should be noted as an eclectic approach. No one path is more important than another. It is also important to realize that for each person with misophonia, their own history, needs, and opinions will be of great importance when deciding how to implement these steps. What is important is that the person with misophonia is experiencing meaningful changes from this advocacy-based approach.

Example Use of the Misophonia Matters Approach

Session 1: Initial appointment. Psychoeducation mixed with learning about the client.

Session 2: Misophonia assessment followed by debriefing and seeing the client's perspective on the assessment.

Session 3: Begin psychoeducation and presenting materials. This step could take several sessions, or as few as one, depending on the prior knowledge of the client.

Session 4: Discussing misophonia with the client and figuring out what their main concerns involve. Useful to share the potential Misophonia Matters pathways and see which they choose.

Session 5: Engaging in the chosen activities with the client. Room should be left for an open discussion on the path and how the client feels about this chosen activity.

Session 6: Repeat pathways until all chosen pathways have been followed. Debrief after each step.

Session 7: Misophonia assessment and debriefing on the therapy process. This might be in later sessions, depending on the specific needs of each client.

Pathways and Overlap

For my approach to misophonia, the pathways are split into sections as a means to sort information. This, however, is not a perfect waypoint, as there is often overlap between sections. For example, advocacy and accommodations are present throughout many steps, and learning to live with misophonia often involves a mixture of psychological, cognitive, and sensory regulation-based skills. It is my belief that a strict adherence to one means of thought is the antithesis to living with misophonia, as we are all individuals with a variety of accumulated experiences, ideas, coping skills, and neurophysiological needs. Regardless of your preferred theory of cognition, each one of us only has one brain and one body.

Advocacy

Central to this method is a focus on advocacy for misophonia. While coping skills and self-regulation skills are taught as part of the approach, there is an emphasis on advocacy at every step of the journey. For example, advocacy can have powerful implications before a person is triggered by misophonia through negotiating boundaries for a person with misophonia, during the misophonic moment by negotiating a way for the person with misophonia to navigate the trigger, and after the misophonic moment by developing practical strategies to change the environment for the person with misophonia for the better.

Negotiations and Communication Skills

Accommodations for misophonia are necessary since the world is often not a place where persons with misophonia (or misokinesia) can interact easily. Examples of places where accommodations are necessary include the home, school (K-college), workplace environments, hobbies, and medical environments. The accommodations needed will depend on what the triggers are and what environments the person with misophonia frequents.

Learning to communicate to others about misophonia is challenging and oftentimes daunting. It can be hard to predict how the other person will react to the knowledge of misophonia, so an advocacy-based psychoeducation approach is a useful tool to have in these moments. Most people do not want to hurt others, but on the flip side, no one wants to be accused of harming somebody else. This paradigm can make bringing up the conversation of misophonia challenging and tedious for all parties involved.

Sensory-Based Skills

Sensory-based skills have been used by occupational therapists for sensory integration, autism, and sensory processing issues for several decades. Using a sensory regulation approach to misophonia can help bring the body and brain together in hopes that the nervous system will be calmed. These skills can be used before going into the misophonic moment, during the moment, and then afterwards to help maintain calm.

Cognitive and Psychological Approaches

Cognitive and psychological approaches for misophonia can be eclectic and do not have to follow a strict course of action. Since no amount of cognitive, psychological, or behavioral approaches will change the presence of misophonia, it is important that we only spend time on activities that are helpful for the individual. There is nothing wrong with one person not "clicking" with a narrative or CBT approach, and it is important that we do not dwell on what *did not help*. Whether this is with the help of a clinician or on your own, coping techniques should never make life worse for the individual with misophonia.

Misophonia Assessment

Measuring misophonia can be done with a self-report. Clinicians can help their clients to fill out this self-report, or it can be completed on its own. While misophonia is not currently in a diagnostic manual, the ability to engage in an assessment serves as a way to validate the concerns of sufferers and shows a scientifically centered result that represents the degree of impairment caused by misophonia.

In all likelihood, more measures on misophonia will be developed as knowledge of the disorder spreads and more researchers become involved. To date, however, the most thorough, reliable, and valid measure that I have seen is the Duke Misophonia Questionnaire (DMQ) (Rosenthal et al., 2021). While there are several subscales, to save time I often focus on page one "Trigger Frequency" of the DMQ which takes stock of an individual's triggers, as well as page eight "Impairment" which is the clinical sub-scale. The full DMQ can provide a more in-depth picture of misophonia and can be found on the Duke CMER website: https://psychiatry.duke.edu/duke-center-misophonia-and-emotion-regulation/misophonia-resources/duke-misophonia-questionnaire

While this assessment does not serve as a diagnosis, it is an important part of understanding the condition and realizing that misophonia sufferers are not making things up, as well as showing that there is a significant degree of impairment that comes with the disorder.

Learning about Misophonia

Rather than our thoughts and emotions controlling our physical and emotional reactions to sensory stimuli, the sensory stimuli and fight-flight reaction are causing the response.

A person with misophonia will hear a sound, and then the brain (amygdala) will conceive this sound as a threat which leads to an emotional (and physiological) response. This is why no amount of "thinking the trigger away" will work; your thought process is not coming into the conversation with your brain until *after* you have been triggered by whatever stimuli is causing the misophonic reaction. Why these sounds are triggering a fight-flight-freeze reaction has not yet been discovered.

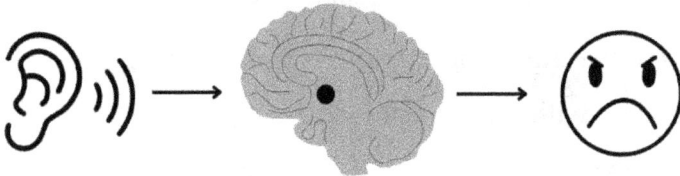

When we stop to think about *why* we are having an emotional reaction, most people do not initially have stories that go alongside triggers. For example, the *first time* we are triggered by something is likely not something that we remember. We may, however, have negative associations of these triggers and times when we were triggered by family and friends—or even specific locations where we were triggered. The emotion, however, comes later than the initial fight-flight-freeze response.

Fight, Flight, Freeze

When the brain and body enter fight-flight-freeze, there are only three responses available to us as a reaction. We can either fight, flee, or completely freeze in response. For misophonia, fight rarely amounts to violence unless in young children, yet there might be thoughts of anger and disgust, or a verbal outburst asking the person to stop (perhaps unkindly). Flight is self-explanatory, since when facing triggers, many with misophonia leave the environment if they can. Freeze tends to be more perplexing for those who are triggered and those around them. Freeze can amount to feeling unable to react or even staring at the triggering offender. Consider this, if you were in the room with a person you do not know who is wielding a knife in your direction—would you take your eyes off the knife?

Fight-flight-freeze is our body's way of helping us identify and deal with threats, and for reasons we do not yet know, misophonia causes this release of adrenaline in the body which causes distress after hearing a trigger sound. Habituation refers to the state where a person becomes accustomed to a state or stimuli. For people with misophonia, habituation is a state that we never achieve as our nervous systems do not become accustomed to the triggering sounds or visuals.

What is the Autonomic Nervous System?
The Autonomic Nervous System (ANS) is a complex part of the body that controls the fight-flight-freeze response, as well as other necessary functions for human existence.

The autonomic nervous system is a component of the peripheral nervous system that regulates involuntary physiologic processes including heart rate, blood pressure, respiration, digestion, and sexual arousal. It contains three anatomically distinct divisions: sympathetic, parasympathetic, and enteric. (Waxenbaum, 2023)

The autonomic nervous system (ANS) is made up of pathways of neurons that control various organ systems inside the body, using many diverse chemicals and signals to maintain homeostasis. It divides into the sympathetic and parasympathetic systems. The sympathetic component is better known as "fight or flight" and the parasympathetic component as "rest and digest." It functions without consconscious control throughout the lifespan of an organism to control cardiac muscle, smooth muscle, and exocrine and endocrine glands, which in turn regulate blood pressure, urination, bowel movements, and thermoregulation. (LeBouef, 2023)

The sympathetic part of the autonomic nervous system is responsible for the fight-flight system, whereas the parasympathetic part is responsible for stopping the fight-flight response. The fight-flight response is first detected by the amygdala, which then alerts the hippocampus to activate the sympathetic nervous system. Once this is activated, adrenaline rushes through the system, elevates the heartrate, and causes what people describe as the "anxious" response. The parasympathetic system is responsible for stopping this response, and thus helps the body reach what many refer to as "calm". The enteric system deals with digestion and will not be touched upon in this book.

While we know that people with misophonia are having a fight-flight response, we do not know *why* this is happening. More rigorous research and brain-based studies will be necessary to fully decipher the origins of misophonia and its reasons for onset. While the nervous system is an important component for understanding misophonia, it can be helpful to avoid getting lost in the weeds of complicated neurophysiological processes, especially given the preliminary status of this research. However, if one is interested in reading more about the brain basis for misophonia, the best place to start is this study by Dr. Sukhbinder Kumar:

Kumar, S., Tansley-Hancock, O., Sedley, W., Winston, J.S., Callaghan, M.F., Allen, M., Cope, T.E., Gander, P.E., Bamiou, D.E., & Griffiths, T.D. (2017). The brain basis for misophonia. *Current Biology,* 27(4).

https://www.sciencedirect.com/science/article/pii/S0960982216315305?via%3Dihub

What is Sensory-Regulation and Self-Regulation?

Sensory regulation is "the ability to select and process sensory information to plan and perform appropriate behaviors" (Piccardi and Gliga, 2022). Rather than our behavior being something that is driven by our cognitive needs, it is instead driven by our neurophysiological and sensory needs (Dunn, 2014). Self-regulation refers to the ability to manage our own physiological states and choose behaviors in accordance with these states (Shanker and

Barker, 2016). For the purpose of this book, when I mention "sensory regulation" I am referring to the ability to calm the nervous system when triggered by sensory stimuli.

Coping with Misophonia

Figuring out what can help with misophonia in the 2020s is a landmine. A quick world wide web search for "treatments for misophonia" will land you thousands of results—some of which are asking for payments for apps, hypnotherapy, or other promised treatments. One time I even found an essential oil blend which *literally claimed to cure misophonia*. There are some options that do offer some help for the condition, but wading through the depths of charlatans to land on a helpful coping skill or treatment becomes unlikely when we consider that Google does not regulate advertisements for treatments, and thus anybody can pay to serve you advertisements, regardless of the ethics.

Tangent aside, coping with misophonia is something that varies from person to person. Each person with misophonia has different variations of triggers, different needs for things that they are unable to live without such as eating dinner with a loved one, and different ideas and opinions on how misophonia impacts their life. This variability does not mean that nothing can help misophonia, but it does mean that any person seeking self-help must consider their own needs specifically.

Part of dealing with the variability of misophonia, at least in my opinion, is developing communication and negotiation skills by way of advocating for yourself or a loved one with misophonia. Through this process, we can move through the world of misophonia and our sensory needs by learning how to adapt and negotiate our way through these uncomfortable moments. For example, no amount of deep breathing exercise will help me to sit in a room with a clicking pen. What could happen is a negotiation that allowed me to avoid sitting in the room in the first place, or the ability to wear earplugs or a sound generator in this room. I will still have misophonia, but I will be able to mitigate this fight-flight-freeze response through a reasonable accommodation which is achieved through advocacy.

It is my firm belief that coping with misophonia is a work of advocacy. In fact, managing most disorders whether neurological, neurophysiological, or psychological requires a degree of advocacy to help cope with the disorder and navigate a world that is not built for your brain chemistry.

Advocacy can be as simple as negotiating with a loved one how you will manage your home lives with your condition, or as complex as engaging in public awareness, writing letters, and influencing policy that impacts misophonia. There is no level of advocacy, however, that is required for misophonia by default.

Before we discuss potential coping skills for misophonia, I think it is important to mention that any life change that you make that helps you cope with misophonia is your own form of coping skill, and so long as it is not maladaptive and harmful, this is a meaningful state of change.

One way to cope is by masking sounds. For misophonia, I often use pink noise (specifically, the sound of mountain rain) as I personally find it the least jarring of noises. Since there is no actual research on the noises of misophonia and why each sound is a trigger, we do not really know enough to say which noise will be most beneficial. I personally prefer a pink noise, but others might do better with brown or white. The research on sound masking is an ever-developing field with little research in general, and none to date on misophonia. The most important part of these sound masking types is that you personally feel calmed and soothed by it. You can even use a combination at different times and find what works for you specifically.

I personally like to combine pink noise with ear plugs. I find that the combination of both blocks most triggers, whilst it also gives me protection from the white noise being too loud and damaging my ears. Noise-cancelling headphones paired with earplugs can work in public. At home, I play pink noise through my speakers in my room as I find wearing earplugs and headphones continuously can give me a headache. While you can purchase devices specifically to play these sounds, Spotify, Amazon Music, and other music stores often have files that you can play on your mobile devices or speakers.

Many people I see (especially parents) worry that misophonia will get worse as a person ages. However, I want to come and tell you that there is no evidence that this is true. In fact, most people seem to stick with the same triggers they have (there are about twenty of them that are common: whistling, chewing, coughing, snoring, etc.).

Misophonia, instead of getting better or worse over time, "waxes and wanes" (Brout, 2021). What this means is that there are times when a person is more troubled by sounds, whilst during other times they can handle them better. If you are stressed during exams, a divorce, or any other life event, then it stands to reason that your nervous system and fight-flight response are going to be completely out of whack too. Similarly, during uplifting life events, misophonia can be on the backburner. For example, I remember misophonia being less of a concern whilst completely in bliss after my partner said "I love you" for the first time. It was an opportune moment to go to a movie theatre (and I think we actually did).

Similarly, avoidance is not going to make triggers better or worse. It is completely okay to take your time and stay at home or wear headphones. There is no reason to believe that people are going to make misophonia worse by avoiding triggers. I for one can say that if I take regular breaks and establish boundaries, then my overall happiness level is much greater!

Misophonia and Visual Triggers

One question I am asked now and then is "how do visual triggers relate to misophonia?" While that is a great question, and one I wish I knew the answer to, it is unfortunately one that we do not know. In 2013, Arjan Schröder proposed the term misokinesia for visual triggers that were present in patients that had misophonia. This term was not meant to coin a new disorder, but more to explain a phenomenon that was not encapsulated by the disorder as it was known at the time (Schröder et al., 2013).

I would like to first start by saying that misokinesia (hatred of movement) is a term that oversimplifies things. As far as the available research is concerned, there is not enough to say if visual triggers are different from misophonia. They might both be related, they could be part of a sensory processing disorder, or they could be two interlinked disorders. The research simply is not there. We also do not know whether or not *all*, *most*, or *some* sufferers also have visual triggers.

We do not yet know if all persons with misophonia also have misokinesia (i.e., they are the same disorder), or if some persons with aversive reactions to sounds (misophonia) do not have an aversion to visuals (misokinesia). It is possible that these aversions happen on a spectrum and are different in each clinical case. This is something that has not yet been researched.

At this time, what I can say is that many in the community, myself included, have reported both visual and auditory triggers that manifest with a similar fight-flight-freeze reaction. For those that do have misokinesia, there is little difference between the nature of the trigger after the outset. Our fight-flight systems are engaged, we feel discomfort, sometimes pain, and then negative emotional effects.

The name "misophonia" is misleading anyways, since we do not "hate" sounds (or visuals), but rather are merely experiencing aversive reactions to the way our brains are processing these stimuli as a threat. Yet, this is the name that the popular press and researchers have clung to and landed upon, so we must accept it for now. In the meantime, it is important to realize that much of the knowledge that we have on both auditory and visual triggers is in the beginning stages of discovery, and nothing is set in stone.

My visual triggers are just as hard to handle as my audial triggers. Sometimes they are worse. I find it nearly impossible to escape a sight in a room. Even when I close my eyes, and even hours or days later, the memory is still there. I want to cry as I think of these triggers. Legs shaking, people swaying, fingers and toes tapping. Even improper grammar has been known to become triggering. Double spacing after periods is so intensely anguishing that I have had to block people from communication.

Having severe visual *and* audial triggers has made life more challenging. The grammar and typing and lighting triggers are so severe that I find it nearly impossible to surf the web, play video games, and even be near Christmas lights.

I have the following visual triggers:

- Two spaces instead of one after a period.
- Use of "u" "r" or "ur" instead of full words.
- You're/your used improperly.
- An overabundance of punctuation, especially "!"
- Legs and arms in places that are strange to me (one leg up, one leg down).
- Arms leaning across car doors.
- Untied shoelaces.
- Effects in video games.
- Bright lights.
- Pinwheels, windmills, and all other "rotating" circles.
- Bags (being swung on an arm).

- Anything flipping or breezing.
- Words used improperly.
- An improper ellipsis (more than three consecutive dots...).
- An overuse of ellipses.
- Chewing (the visual, no sound necessary; actually I am bothered more by the look than the sound).

For me, visual triggers have been harder to explain because even our own community media does not do enough to explain. Of course, I cannot fault us; there simply is not enough data (scientific or otherwise). Sometimes it is hard to handle visual triggers because I cannot wear earplugs for my eyes. I suppose I could wear a blindfold, but this has impractical applications. The important takeaway here is that visual triggers have been reported by the community and may or may not be associated with the same brain processes as misophonia.

The Eclectic Nature of Coping Skills

Whether a therapist for misophonia uses a narrative-based approach, a cognitive behavioral approach, or family systems theory—or all of the above and more, is essentially a moot point. Coping skills for misophonia are custom tailored to the individual and are very specific to the person or family at hand. With that said, the use of the words *coping skills* rather than *treatment* is deliberate on my part. The reason for this is that misophonia is not something that can be mitigated entirely, and therefore the clinicians that are helping persons with misophonia should be mindful that the word treatment has connotations of alleviating a disorder entirely. Instead, coping with misophonia surrounds the misophonic moment rather than alleviates it entirely.

No amount of narrative therapy will change that misophonia exists for the person suffering with the disorder. Even if the word *treatment* is necessary for academic or insurance purposes, this should never be used to confuse sufferers of misophonia into thinking that a particular approach is going to lead to a mitigation of the triggers.

The words *coping skills* are far more honest when it comes to the "treatment" of misophonia as they offer a more nuanced approach. It is also important to realize that not all persons with misophonia will react to a narrative approach or a behavioral approach and it is up to individual practitioners to choose the most appropriate coping skills for their client. Even as I look into interventions for misophonia from the perspective of a new clinician, I am often worried that the usage of words by other practitioners can have harmful connotations.

Your expectations, or those of your client, for coping with misophonia are important going into any plan for coping skills. Coming into coping skills while understanding that misophonia is a condition that we live with, and not something that we can completely eradicate, is important. While this can be hard to hear, it is very important to realize that there are no treatments for misophonia, and especially no treatments that can erase the condition entirely. Instead, our expectations should shift to learning to live with misophonia and learning to live in a world that is not always accommodating for misophonia.

Part 2: Advocacy and Explaining

Why Does Advocacy Matter?

In a busy world, it can be daunting to imagine dedicating your time through volunteering or spreading awareness of misophonia. With that said, advocating for yourself, your loved ones, and others around you, is one of the most important ways that we can change the world. Advocacy does not have to be flashy campaigns or full-time dedication. Educating others and highlighting resources is an important part of advocacy. Fighting for your own accommodations or those of your client is a means of advocacy that not only helps an individual, but also the greater population as these accommodations become more widespread and accepted. Advocacy is a series of actions, and over time, even the smallest of these actions add up to meaningful change. Knowledge is power, and this is especially true with a newer lesser-known disorder such as misophonia.

Advocacy can help us change the world around us and is powerful in the everyday lives of persons with misophonia. For example, through advocacy we can help teachers, doctors, and even researchers understand the needs of the misophonia community, and thus help guide the narrative that leads to better accommodations, research, and acceptance of persons with misophonia and sensory disorders.

Learning to Self-Advocate

Self-advocacy is the process in which persons with misophonia learn to explain misophonia to others, negotiate accommodations, and become aware of their boundaries when it comes to triggering environments. Some persons with misophonia worry that asking for accommodations will be met with resistance or even think that they should not ask for accommodations at all because it is "their problem". It is my belief that this is not true and that persons with misophonia deserve to live enriched lives without being constantly dysregulated.

Maladaptive versus Adaptive Coping Mechanisms

People with misophonia and sensory integration issues in general (think autism, sensory processing, etc.) create ways to cope without even thinking about it. Some of these coping methods are adaptive and some of them are maladaptive.

A maladaptive coping mechanism is when we find ways to cope that are counterproductive to the thing we are trying to cope with or otherwise harmful for health. Common maladaptive behaviors are unhealthy foods, cigarettes, drug misuse, alcohol abuse, gambling, and self-harm. This is not an exhaustive list, but rather highlights that maladaptive coping mechanisms are not only unhelpful long-term, but often harmful.

On the other hand, an adaptive coping mechanism is something that is both helpful for misophonia and anxiety and also beneficial for the long-term health of the individual. Common examples of adaptive coping mechanisms are engaging in exercise, yoga, a well-balanced nutritious diet, drinking water, and spending time in nature.

In an audio interview in 2015, Dr. Stephen Porges noted that clients with misophonia often have a higher incidence of maladaptive behaviors (https://www.misophoniainternational.com/the-polyvagal-theory-2/). More research is necessary for confirming this phenomenon, but it is unsurprising to me to think that people with misophonia who never learned how to regulate—or even *what regulation is*—are not gravitating toward adaptive coping skills for misophonia. It is also possible that because misophonia is hardwired so deep in the brain that the person did try traditional adaptive coping mechanisms such as eating right, exercise, and yoga, and were met with a crushing defeat—they still had misophonia, so why bother?

Is Avoidance Adaptive or Maladaptive?

Whether or not *avoidance* is a maladaptive coping mechanism is something that psychiatrists and psychologists debate. In the view of some authors, avoidance is a maladaptive behavior because it can hinder social events and learning engagement, and thus should be remedied. This view is simplistic and does not account for the lack of habituation that is shown in persons with misophonia. When we think of misophonia through the lens of sensory regulation and the fight-flight-freeze response, it is only natural that a person with misophonia would want to *avoid* a trigger or leave the room when it happens. The easiest way to not be distressed is to not be in the presence of the stressor!

Whether or not *avoidance* is maladaptive or adaptive depends on numerous factors, and almost all of them are up to the individual and by extension their families. Social expectations are largely cultural and whether something like family dinner is something to be adapted to and coped with or something that can be avoided will be situational. For some, the distress at mealtimes is so great that even the cultural will to eat dinner with one's family is not enough to overcome the urge to flee. It is important to not judge too harshly in these situations—even if it is yourself that you are judging.

There is a degree in which avoidance is a maladaptive coping mechanism, and that degree is whatever line the person with misophonia has drawn in the sand. For some, there are hard boundaries that cannot be crossed such as restaurants or movie theatres. For others, these lines are more nuanced and some days they can handle it and other days they cannot. This variance is to be expected when we consider self-regulation and remember that misophonia varies based on the physiological, cognitive, and emotional needs of a person, and not just on hard assumptions.

Of course, if a person with misophonia has become overly withdrawn, lonely, or is avoiding relationships with their friends and family altogether, this is a maladaptive behavior. However, it is possible that it is not necessarily misophonia causing this behavior, but rather a lack of accommodations and safety in the relationship which helps the person with misophonia stay present. Unfortunately, some triggers cannot be covered (such as the sound of a person's voice), so this can become tricky in these scenarios.

The answer to the question this chapter sought to answer—"Is avoidance adaptive or maladaptive?"—is that it entirely depends on how often the person is avoiding, why they are avoiding, and whether or not it is leading to more distress for the individual who is doing the avoiding. While that answer might seem convoluted, it is also one that might change through negotiating accommodations and developing coping mechanisms.

Adaption not Manipulation

For parents of misophonic children, romantic partners, friends, and educators, some traits of misophonia might look to them as manipulative behavior. For those with misophonia, when we are in fight-flight-freeze mode and dysregulated, our brains and bodies are telling us to do *anything* to stop the trigger—just as I imagine one would in any scenario that the brain and body have earmarked as a threat. It should be no surprise that when faced with an extremely aversive reaction to sounds (or visuals), a person with misophonia would go to extreme lengths to stop the noise. Examples of this might be coming up with alternative explanations to try and force the event not to happen. For example, one might say they cannot go out because they have to do x, y, or z. Perhaps a partner goes to great lengths to avoid date night, even cancelling with excuses. Maybe the person comes up with a story for why something cannot be in their presence—for example, they might respond to gum chewers by saying that they are allergic to the smell. A parent with misophonia may tell their child that their loud chewing is rude, which is socially true in many circumstances, but this might not be the motivation for the request.

On the surface, these behaviors might seem manipulative. The definition of manipulate is to "control or influence a person or situation cleverly, unfairly, or unscrupulously." The key point here is "unfairness" or "unscrupulously". For persons with misophonia, it is not control of the other person that they want to achieve, but rather to alleviate or prevent a misophonic reaction. This behavior is adaptive. People with misophonia are accustomed to being ignored, ridiculed, and told that their condition is not real. Even those who feel supported might deal with guilt for asking others to stop a behavior due to misophonia, and thus might rationalize an excuse that is to them more "logical" even if the receiving party suspects that misophonia is the cause.

An important part of misophonia is learning to self-advocate and adapt with the condition. However, for some, it can be harder, especially if the other party is not open to learning about their condition or accommodating it. Instead of thinking people with misophonia are manipulative, let us consider that maybe they are just trying to avoid an unpleasant neurophysiological reaction, rather than controlling the person making the trigger for nefarious reasons.

How to Ask People to Stop Triggering You Without Being Rude

As a person with misophonia, I am constantly uncomfortable and feel like the world is against me. I do not want to feel this way, but it is a fact that many of the sounds that trigger misophonia and the visuals that trigger misokinesia are ones that are made by other people or by machinery used by other people. Some of these include lawnmowers, loud base music, rattling car engines and exhausts, and whistling, among others. I am not even mentioning chewing or sniffling because these are sounds that I genuinely think we cannot even bring up to strangers since they are necessary to life.

I have politely asked people in public to stop whistling. The way I explain this often goes like this:

> *Me: Excuse me, I am so sorry to ask, I have a hearing condition and I was wondering if you could please stop whistling? Again, I am so sorry to ask.*

Yes, the Canadian in me says sorry twice. I hate inconveniencing people in general so asking them to change their actions to suit me is something I genuinely do not want to do. Yet, by asking politely, I have noticed that oftentimes people are happy to adjust. I will say that sometimes I feel far too aggravated and dysregulated to ask a person to stop, so the avoidance and resentment of my fellow human beings starts to come into play.

I think the key to not being rude is to ensure that you are being polite and mindful of the other person, acknowledging that what they are doing is not wrong and that you are not entitled to their compliance, yet asking in a way that is kind and polite. If the person does not stop the behavior, unfortunately there is very little that can be done, so hopefully you do not have to be around them too often. If this is somebody you must be around every day (such as a colleague), then it would be reasonable to escalate the matter in my opinion, especially since (and only after) you tried to calmly and politely address the subject. This could be achieved by discussing options with your boss, consulting your human resources department, or asking your therapist to write you a note explaining misophonia.

How To Explain Misophonia

Do you want to explain misophonia to others, but have trouble bringing it up?

When you know that you must tell someone about your disorder (especially trying to explain misophonia), it can be stressful—the anxiety, fear, and anticipation can be enough to keep your mouth firmly shut and continue your suffering. Instead, I suggest that people with misophonia learn how to explain misophonia and negotiate boundaries and accommodations. You may want to adjust the conversation depending on whom you are talking to, but these tips should help you when thinking about how to act, what to do, and what to say. It is a good idea to make sure that you and your client are not triggered at the time of the conversation. During a trigger, anger is heightened, and the person with misophonia will perceive the person triggering them as a threat. If the person with misophonia comes to this conversation with a loud or accusatory voice, this will set off the nervous system of the second party, thus leading to two angry dysregulated persons trying to communicate.

Instead, consider the following for explaining misophonia to others:

- Prepare yourself with research and website links that can be helpful to explain misophonia to the person you are about to approach. Make sure they will understand that it is a real condition and that you are serious.
- Keep your mood stress-free and ensure that you are relaxed beforehand. Try to have a bath, some tea, some light television, or something you enjoy before you have the conversation. If you are stressed or tired, then the conversation may go sour quickly. It is important that you are in a good mood for the conversation.
- Choose a location in which you know there will be little to no triggers. Try to be somewhere in which you and the other individual are both comfortable. If this is impossible, try to become familiar with the place beforehand (such as talking to the person in their office beforehand, and asking if you can meet another day, when you have more time, or are prepared).

During

During the conversation, your aim should be to keep it positive and informative. You should provide examples of what triggers you, even if they are not the same ones that trigger you in the environment with the person. It is important they understand that it is not just when you are around this person, and that this disorder impacts several aspects of your life. Do not make it all about them.

- It may be helpful to print off articles that explain misophonia. Since research is minimal, some of the websites listed at the end of this book can be helpful for learning about misophonia.
- If the person triggers you during the conversation, identify it but not in an aggressive manner. Excuse yourself and explain that what they are doing is one of the things that causes a reaction. Politely ask if they can stop or if there is a way they can adjust their behavior. Make sure they understand you are not blaming them, but that the condition is serious.
- Do not apologize for misophonia or make excuses. Say that it is a neurophysiological condition and that you have it. Be matter of fact and explain that unfortunately there is no cure.
- Discuss a way that you can let them know you are being triggered, without being offensive or turning to anger. If the conversation starts to go sour, or the person does not understand—excuse yourself. Do not let anger turn into a confrontation. Explain that you were merely explaining your feelings, and that this has a huge impact on your life. Leave before it becomes more serious, since often leaving is a statement of its own.

Afterwards

Chances are that after you explain misophonia to another person, they will still trigger you. It can be hard for a person to recondition things that they are used to doing, and even harder for them to remember. Unlike you, this person does not deal with misophonia on a day-in-day-out basis, so it is unlikely that it is something they consider regularly. Do not blame them for this, and do not hold it against them. Unless the person is trying to trigger you and disregards your feelings entirely, you should be mindful that they are probably not out to get you, and that this is merely a reaction from misophonia.

- If you have to remind them that they are triggering you, be polite.
- Leave the room and if they ask why, explain that you are being triggered.
- Try to remain positive; do not engage when you are angry.

Boss or Administration

Misophonia is challenging to discuss with others. Your boss should be a person that you trust and that you can approach with issues that involve your work performance and comfort in the workplace. For some people, their boss is intimidating and a person they would rather not confront. Either way, it is best to go into this conversation prepared. You should explain how misophonia is a neurophysiological condition that can be mitigated, although there is little information and no cure as of yet. Ask your boss if there is anything they can do to help and assure them that you are committed to the job and are asking for the betterment of not just you but your performance. If your boss is unsupportive, you should be equipped with the laws reflecting accessibility in your region.

Coworkers

Coworkers can be tricky. You have to play nice when you have a job. This is especially worrisome for those that work in an office environment. Many workplaces are starting to allow snacking on the job, and this causes many triggers. Being polite can go a long way with other workers, no matter the situation. However, sometimes coworkers are unwilling to stop something that they believe is "their right". Approach the coworker when you are not triggered and inform them that you have a medical condition and ask them if they would be willing to help accommodate you. If they are unwilling to help, inform your boss. You should already have told your boss about your misophonia and discussed the possibility of accommodations. If you are lucky, you may be able to convince your boss to speak with your coworker. Remind everyone involved how misophonia is a neurophysiological condition that you cannot control.

Friends

I now refuse to spend time recreationally with people who do not respect my misophonia. It was a hard adjustment at first, but the people who truly care about me are able to respect my condition. Friendship, like dating, should be based on mutual understanding and trust. You should not have to pressure your friend to respect your needs and wishes, and your friend should not feel attacked by your sudden rage at noises or visuals. Be sure to explain to your friend that you do not mean anything by your displeasure, and that you truly value their time and your relationship. Ask if you can have gatherings in trigger-neutral zones and plan your outings so that the possibility of a trigger is minimal. This can be hard, since many friendships involve activities that involve noises or visual stimuli. Try to pick outings that have noises that you are comfortable with. For example, I am fine with the sounds of bowling balls and pins crashing. Bowling is a great way to hang out with friends because most of the people I can see are standing (which means they are not shaking any body parts) and the rest of the facility is usually dark. A great friend will understand that you are not doing this to be nitpicky and will want to make you feel better. However, you must understand that they have emotions too, and that you should try not to attack them when triggered.

Family

Those nearest and dearest are often the worst triggers. We spend so much time with our loved ones, and in general, we seem less forgiving when it comes to their behaviors. Day in and day out with the same people can be stressful for any situation. Even if you do not live with a family member, the intensity of the relationship can still cause misophonia triggers to be worse. My first ever "trigger person" that I knew was my mother. At first, every time she shook her foot, it was a major fight. We are talking about volcanic eruptions on both sides. You did not want to be there when she played music and when she sang. I know it is not her fault that she does these things, and they never used to bother me. Misophonia does not always make sense.

Romantic Partners

Romantic relationships such as marriages and partnerships are very similar to family relationships, except we are discussing primarily adult relationships and not relationships between family members that might range significantly in age and cognitive functioning. With that said, romantic relationships are often very complex, and that is part of the reason why I am also working on a guide specific to marriage/relationships and misophonia. I am writing these books at the same time, so whichever comes out first will be up to the universe!

Example: I often find that when I try to talk to my husband about misophonia, I become flustered and upset rather than calmly engaging in a dialog about misophonia.

Roommates
Like family, these people are there on a day-to-day basis. However, unlike family, there may not be enough of a personal relationship that you can confront the individual in a positive manner. Sometimes our living arrangements are out of our control. You may be living in a dorm room, an apartment, or another communal situation. Money and other uncontrollable forces often lead to the necessity of living with an acquaintance or even a stranger. Ideally, we would never live with someone with whom we did not have a good relationship. Unfortunately, reality is not always a perfect picture. If you are going to be living with a new person, you should discuss your misophonia before moving in. Try to be sure that the person you are going to live with truly understands your needs and establish ground rules. Explain that you are not trying to dictate to them and that you are merely suffering from a neurophysiological

condition. If they or a current roommate do not respect these ground rules, perhaps you should consider a different living arrangement if possible. Living with your triggers should only be a last resort. While you cannot avoid triggers in every aspect of your life, the home should be a neutral place where you can calmly relax for the sake of your health and your sanity.

Script for Explaining Misophonia to Strangers

The key to this exercise is to be polite and not put blame on the offending trigger. By asking for help and staying neutral when asking for accommodation, you are much less likely to anger the recipient of the request. In a perfect world, accommodations would be far easier to ask for, but in the world we live in it is important to mitigate frustration when explaining the disorder.

Sample Script

Script: Hello, excuse me I am so sorry to ask you this, but would you mind not doing [trigger here], I have a sensory disorder and it causes me distress. I would really appreciate it if you would be willing to help me.

Write your own script

_____

_____

_____

_____

_____

_____

Explaining Misophonia to People You See Often

This exercise has reminders for the steps to take when explaining misophonia to your boss, friends/co-workers, family, and other persons who are in your life on a regular basis.

- Only explain misophonia for the first time when you are not triggered if possible.

- Bring the results of a misophonia assessment and/or accommodations list in letter form to the conversation (most helpful for work but can also help for some doubtful families).

- Focus on the way the trigger makes you feel and the sound/visual, NOT the person making the sound/visual.

- Acknowledge that accommodating misophonia can be hard and express gratitude when you are accommodated.

- Provide resources such as the Printout Guides on the IMF website, links to scientific articles, and other explanations that are formalized.

Why is Misophonia Triggered Worse by People You Love?

Since we spend more time with our friends and family, it should be no surprise that their noises (and visuals) become some of our worst triggers. It can still be baffling to come to terms with the fact that our own mothers, fathers, siblings, or friends are causing us distress. It is important to note that while people we are close to may be our worst triggers, this does not mean that it is because of anything they or you have done.

Sensory information is cumulative. Because of this, each time we are triggered we become more overwhelmed, and we may react more quickly to someone around us. We are also more likely to trust that a family member or a friend will still love us if we overreact! Another reason loved ones may trigger us falls more along the lines of our brain makeup concerning our memories. The more a person triggers us, the more likely we are to associate them with the triggering stimuli. Unlike someone without misophonia, we do not "get used" to a sound or experience. Instead, it becomes a never-ending nightmare. If you are anxious or tense around a person, you may be more likely to store triggers in memory. If a person is a trigger, you should try to handle the situation as calmly as possible. It is best to leave explanations of your disorder for when you are calm. Escalating the situation is unlikely to repair the damage, and the negativity can just make your disorder worse.

While we cannot always avoid trigger sounds, it can sometimes be best to leave the situation when your nervous system gets triggered, since you can sometimes become calm by avoiding the situation for a brief period of time. Leaving the situation can be helpful to readjust your nervous system. This can be hard for many, but it is something that can be adapted to over time.

On some days, triggers may be worse than others. This can be confusing for people with the disorder. On some days, we can handle some of the triggers surrounding us, and on other days the drop of a pin can bring us to a full-swung panic. Your physiological arousal is worse when you are anxious, already in a bad mood, sick, or simply tired. With this in mind, it is important that we consider our health before going into a situation. While you should not keep yourself away from fun activities, you should not feel guilty about needing more "alone time".

Misophonia and Family Life

Our family is often the first group of people that we are triggered by, and often people with misophonia report this to be the most intense group that they are triggered by as time goes on. By nature of spending more time with our family, it makes sense that we anticipate them triggering us. After all, unlike a stranger, I have historical data residing in my fight-flight-freeze system that tells me the exact likelihood that a trigger will emanate from a loved one. On Amazon a wonderful guide for parents of children with misophonia can be found which is authored by Dr. Jennifer Jo Brout and which is titled "A Parent's Guide to Misophonia: Regulate, Reason, Reassure". I recommend this guide in particular for families with young children that have misophonia, as Dr. Brout has firsthand experience both as a sufferer of misophonia and as a mother who raised a child with misophonia.

There are numerous considerations that make family life advocacy and negotiations more challenging. Unlike jobs or schools, there are no hard and fast accessibility rules that apply to all families. No two families have the same culture, expectations, and values. As families learn about misophonia and begin to negotiate what is acceptable in their own family framework, there might be points of contention that are directly in conflict with belief systems and values that existed before misophonia even came into the equation. This is not to say that a certain family culture is right or wrong, but merely that it is something to take into account when accommodating misophonia.

Example: A family has eaten dinner together every night for generations. This has become a tradition for grandparents, children, and then grandchildren. For this family, dinnertime is a cultural tradition that is enshrined in the fabric of the family. However, the youngest grandchild has a misophonic reaction to chewing and becomes distressed at mealtimes. How will this family negotiate the child's distress while also honoring the importance of mealtime?

This is a question that countless families across the globe must consider when it comes to misophonia. I personally do not have the answer, as this is something that must be negotiated by the family through the lens of their beliefs and worldview. As a person who comes from a family that did not hold family dinnertime in high esteem other than on holidays, I might personally decide that the child eating dinner with the family is of little importance, but for another family this may not be the appropriate answer. Perhaps instead this family could consider adaptive accommodations such as headphones and earplugs.

Family advocacy can extend to family members outside of the immediate sphere, including members like grandparents, cousins, and the extended family if the person with misophonia interacts with these family members in a way where misophonia becomes a point of contention.

Examples of family advocacy

- Choosing a family event night that does not involve a trigger, such as board games, a family walk, or an activity that does not have eating (if this is the main trigger).
- Having the child or adult with misophonia eat in another room during mealtimes, whilst engaging in other family activities during the night (i.e. cooking, conversation afterwards).
- Modifying the environment to help the person with misophonia feel comfortable, such as by having music playing or a place where the misophonic person can eat in the corner of the table with view/sound obstructed.
- Negotiating which triggers are necessary and which triggers are unnecessary, such as by not allowing whistling, gum-chewing, or tapping fingers at family events.

The above list is non-exhaustive. Every family will have examples of their own negotiations and should create their own lists that consider their family makeup. One problem that might arise in families is when another member of the family has a comorbid condition that directly interferes with the triggers of the misophonic family member. In these cases, it is challenging to determine reasonable negotiations that consider each family member equally.

Example: One family member is triggered by legs jiggling. This is very distressing for the person with misophonia, putting them into fight-flight-freeze. Another family member, however, has restless leg syndrome and cannot help shaking their leg regularly. How might this family come to an arrangement that considers both conditions equally?

The above example serves to highlight how challenging these negotiations can become in a real-world scenario. Neither family member is trying to harm the other, nor can they control their fight-flight-freeze-reaction or their leg-shaking. Communication between the two family members could be helpful in this instance. The family member with restless leg syndrome and the misophonic family member could negotiate when it is reasonable for one or the other to leave the room, or the person with misophonia could find a way to "block" the visual trigger, such as a pillow wall when watching a movie. No answer to this question will be perfect, nor is there an answer that can be mandated. The key to handling these scenarios is that there is a collaborative effort and dialog that does not diverge into either party blaming the other.

Creating a Family Genogram

Genograms are a tool often used in Bowenian Family Systems Theory (Ungvarsky, 2022), and they may be helpful for families learning about their family history as it relates to misophonia and relationships between family members. Genograms are a way for therapists working with families, or individual families on their own, to record cognitively relevant family associations over generations. Genograms take effort and can be emotionally difficult to process, yet this is due to their enormous power when it comes to putting down on paper the history of a family. The members of the family involved in creating a genogram do not necessarily have to be all of the family, but rather this can be a useful tool for parents or misophonic members of the family to understand important connections and history that might be making it harder to negotiate misophonia. For example, the above scenario of restless leg syndrome and misophonia could be charted via a genogram.

You can use an online template for a genogram or download Genopro as a free trial to make a genogram. However, there is no reason to buy software for this exercise, as you can also use a piece of paper (or Bristol board). If you are working with small children, you could decorate your genogram with photographs if you like. For the purpose of the example below, I sketched a conflict where my father does not accept misophonia. The red dotted bar indicates a conflict in a genogram.

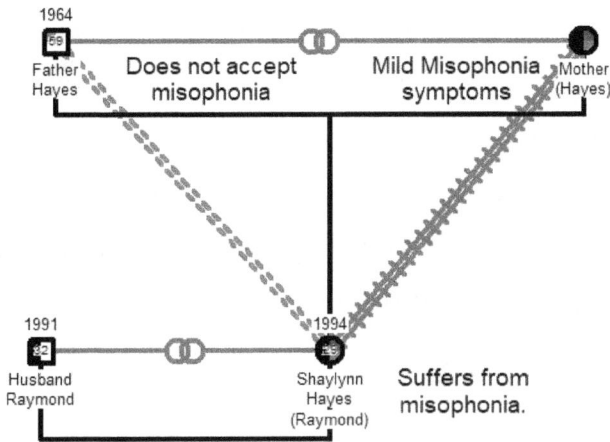

The symbols for genograms can be confusing to learn at first, but it is important to remember that this is not a perfect exercise, but merely to help the family understand their dynamics. Important information to include in a genogram include family conflicts, genetic conditions (such as links where multiple family members have misophonia), and conditions that each family member has such as our example of restless leg syndrome and misophonia. For a comprehensive guide on genogram symbols, you can use the in-depth guide from Edraw:

www.edrawsoft.com/genogram/genogram-symbols.html

You could also look into this software to help with your

genogram: https://www.wingeno.org/#windows

   If you and your family choose to use a genogram, you should remember that the exercise itself should not cause conflict, but merely be used to highlight emotional and genetic relationships that exist in the family. Bowenian theory ascribes to the idea that if one family member makes a change, the entire unit will be changed. Genograms are a tool for understanding the family unit as a whole, and thus can be helpful for identifying areas where negotiation or reflection are necessary.

Family Advocacy Reminder Sheet

- Choosing a family event night that does not involve a trigger, such as board games, a family walk, or an activity that does not involve eating (if this is the main trigger).
- Having the child or adult with misophonia eat in another room during mealtimes, whilst engaging in other family activities during the night (i.e. cooking, conversation afterwards).
- Modifying the environment to help the person with misophonia feel comfortable, such as by having music playing or a place where the misophonic person can eat in a corner of the table with view/sound obstructed.
- Negotiating which triggers are necessary and which triggers are unnecessary, such as by not allowing whistling, gum-chewing, or tapping fingers at family events.

Advocacy in Technology

Advocacy in technology is a daily struggle for many people with misophonia and misokinesia. Blinking lights, beeping UIs, autoplaying videos and gifs, and blinking cursors are some of the things that we are regularly faced with. Unfortunately, many developers are unaware of misophonia/misokinesia, and we are in the wild west for accommodations for these triggers. Advocating for technological change is an ever-evolving part of misophonia advocacy and is something that the International Misophonia Foundation takes seriously. We regularly contact companies such as Discord, Apple, and Android in the hope that our community needs will be heard and that changes will be made for these areas of accessibility.

One way you can help is if you have a trigger that is happening due to your misophonia/misokinesia, then you can contact the app developer to try and alert them to the problem. This helps you advocate for yourself and others. You can also email me at shaylynn@misophoniafoundation.com and I will add your accessibility requirement to our list of developer goals for advocacy.

How to ask a company to make a change based on accessibility

For your email, I suggest making the subject something like "Accessibility Issue" so that developers know that you are contacting them about accessibility. Normally, many companies hold accessibility/disability services higher on their chain of requests than general inquiries. For your email, explain the accessibility issue such as your trigger or which part of their service causes the trigger, and follow up with links if you would like to provide more information on the issue at hand. Below is an example of an email for an accessibility issue in Google's Android operating system.

Subject: Accessibility Issue
To Whom It May Concern,
I am contacting you about an accessibility issue in the Android phone system. I have a disorder called misophonia/misokinesia wherein sounds/visuals cause a fight-flight-freeze reaction. Your system has a blinking "|" cursor during text input that cannot be disabled at a system level. For persons with misokinesia, this is hard to cope with. Please consider addressing this accessibility issue. You can find more information about the condition here: https://www.misophoniainternational.com/misokinesia/ Thank you for your time.
Sincerely,
Your Name

Advocating in your Own Life

The way we live our lives is the most effective means of enacting change that we have. Advocating for misophonia is simultaneously as easy as breathing and as hard as breathing while you have a chest cold. What I mean to say is that self-advocacy becomes a regular part of your day-to-day life, and yet it is exhausting and draining. Much of my coping with misophonia and self-advocacy is mundane. I return emails, ask my partner to please stop making a noise or close his office door, and slap on noise cancelling headphones when lawnmowers start outside my window.

Coping and advocating go together. I advocate for myself so that I can cope better. When I let somebody know about misophonia or my needs, such as not shaking their leg or clicking their pen, I am self-advocating with the desire of coping. Initially, I became a misophonia advocate because I wanted to help others understand the condition. While I love helping people learn how to cope with misophonia, my initial purpose was to increase awareness so that I could more easily navigate the world around me.

Before, During, and After

How one copes with misophonia varies at numerous times of their life, and even during various times during the misophonic moment. The following section will discuss ways to cope with misophonia specifically before you are triggered, during the moments you are triggered, and then after you are triggered. The mix of cognitive and psychological approaches and advocacy is not something that follows a strict path. Instead, all three are providing their influence throughout each part of the process. Misophonia is not linear as we are living breathing people who are trying to cope in a world that is not sensory friendly.

Before

Before the "misophonic" moment, one can utilize sensory regulation to try and stay calm in anticipation of going into the moment. The *misophonia checklist* is also something you can utilize to ensure that you are going into a situation prepared. It can also be helpful to consider advocacy-based approaches to preparing for these scenarios. For example, if you know that there might be triggers in the dentistry waiting room, you can call ahead and ask to sit in a different area so that you will be calmer for the experience. Before the misophonic moment, proactivity is your friend.

During

During the misophonic moment is the most difficult part of coping with misophonia. No amount of proactivity, psychoeducation, or coping skills will change the initial fight-flight-freeze reaction that happens when we are faced with triggers. I am not saying this so that you feel hopeless, but rather so that you are aware that misophonia is not something that we can simply overcome. Usually, during the misophonic moment is not the best time to teach people about misophonia. However, if you are in a situation where you must stay (such as a classroom or medical clinic), it might be prudent to explain briefly misophonia and ask the person if they would be willing to accommodate. In a public space, this is not always possible, and thus preparing with earplugs, earphones, and other tools can be a helpful way to avoid this occurrence.

After

Sensory regulation and cognitive coping skills can be used after the misophonic moment to calm down. Depending on your circumstances, you could utilize the reflection activity to consider how you would do something differently in another misophonic moment (for example, being more assertive, preparing ahead of time, etc.). For sensory regulation, utilizing steps outlined in the Sensory Diet are a useful way to calm down. There is no perfect way to cope, so it is necessary to pick and choose what is helpful for each individual.

Part 3: Accommodations and Negotiations

Misophonia Matters

Misophonia Accommodations

Before we can discuss how to negotiate misophonia accommodations, we must establish what accommodations are specifically. Misophonia accommodations are of course dependent on the needs of the individuals and their triggers, but the following lists will serve as examples of accommodations in various scenarios. For the purpose of potential accommodations, I will include both visual and auditory triggers. Each accommodation is offered as a suggestion; their viability is up to the individual, the parents of a child with misophonia, and the clinician working with a person with misophonia.

Family Accommodations

Family accommodations are often dependent on the environment and are quite nuanced. However, this list serves as an example of what those accommodations might be:

- Wearing noise-cancelling headphones.
- Wearing earplugs.
- Eating family dinners in separate areas.
- Family bonding activities that do not involve food (board games, nature walks, etc.).
- A place in the house where the person with misophonia can retreat.

School Accommodations

School accommodations refer to accommodations for ages from kindergarten to college level:

- Wearing noise-cancelling headphones.
- Wearing earplugs.
- The ability to leave class if overstimulated.
- Online schooling if misophonia is impeding learning.
- A smaller and less overwhelming class.
- No eating in class if possible.
- A set seat/desk in the area where the person is most comfortable.

Work Accommodations

When negotiating with human resources departments and managers, people with misophonia might ask for some of the following accommodations. This is dependent on whether or not it is feasible in their position. Some people with misophonia are adaptive and choose lines of work based on their triggers. The following may be helpful:

- Wearing noise-cancelling headphones.
- Wearing earplugs.
- A private office or cubicle away from others.
- The ability to work from home.
- A job that allows for flexibility in hours.
- No eating in meetings.

Public Accommodations

Public accommodation is not possible in the same way as other accommodations. For example, for the most part we cannot dictate which stores play which music or have specialized shopping trips. Public accommodations are more individually driven by proactively finding ways to cope with misophonia. Here are some suggestions:

- Wearing noise-cancelling headphones.
- Wearing earplugs.
- In waiting room situations, having a family member or friend wait in the room for you and text when it is your turn.
- Using a delivery or online ordering service to limit time in shopping environments.

Accommodations at Schools and Universities

The following is an interview with Dr. Ali Danesh regarding accommodations for misophonia at schools and universities, based on his academic paper on the subject. This interview is reprinted with permission from Dr. Danesh.

Could you tell us a bit about yourself and your work?
I have been working with children and adults with decreased sound tolerance disorders such as hyperacusis and misophonia for many years. In a paper that we published a few years ago we looked at the underlying physiologic, psychologic, neurologic, and audiologic features in misophonia. The research by the scientists show that misophonia is a unique phenomenon occurring within the brain that results in significant reaction to certain sounds. Children and adults with this condition usually do not show significant disturbance of their mental health. However, being exposed to acoustical triggers such as chewing, and other biologic sounds can generate significant emotional and cognitive reactions. These reactions in turn can limit the person's productivity, participation, and progress in both academic and daily life environments.

What has your work in Misophonia been on?
We have emphasized the role of educators on the academic presence and existence of students with misophonia. It was noticed that those with misophonia have a tendency to leave school or limit their participation. We wanted to know how we can keep the students in the schools and be responsible to their needs as academicians.

You published a study on Misophonia accommodations in college—what was your experience with this?
As I mentioned earlier our goal of the research was to find ways to keep students participating in the classroom. The main idea of the research was to explore if the university faculty members know about misophonia and whether they are aware or not, would they provide accommodations for students who cannot stay in a classroom because of certain sound triggers such as chewing. The results of the study showed that although many of the faculty did not know about misophonia, the majority of them had no objection in providing accommodations such as classroom eating rules, quiet rooms for exams, and use of earplugs or personal noise generators if necessary. This complies with the idea of "no child left behind" and it should be the mission for every teacher who interacts with students with disabilities including those who suffer from misophonia.

Do you think accommodations for Misophonia could be harmful?

There is no evidence that accommodations for children and adults with misophonia in the academic environment can cause any harm to students. In our university the office of student accessibility services (SAS) provides support for students with misophonia and has never received any complaints from those who received accommodations!

The remainder of this section includes worksheets for reasonable and unreasonable requests, negotiating boundaries, a sample accommodation letter, and deciding on activities that are alternatives to triggers.

Reminder List of Potential Misophonia Accommodations

- Wearing noise-cancelling headphones.
- Wearing earplugs.
- Calmly asking the triggering person if they would accommodate misophonia.
- Eating family dinners in separate areas.
- Family bonding activities that do not involve food (board games, nature walks, etc.).
- A place in the house where the person with misophonia can retreat.
- The ability to leave class if overstimulated.
- Online schooling if misophonia is impeding learning.
- A smaller and less overwhelming class.
- No eating in class if possible.
- A set seat/desk in the area where the person is most comfortable.
- A private office or cubicle away from others.
- The ability to work from home.
- A job that allows for flexibility in hours.
- No eating in meetings.
- In waiting room situations, having a family member or friend wait in the room for you and text when it is your turn.
- Using a delivery or online ordering service to limit time in shopping environments.

Communication Exercise

How would you explain misophonia to a person who has
never heard of it?

_____

_____

_____

_____

If the person you are explaining misophonia to does not
believe you, what would you say?

_____

_____

_____

_____

Was there a time in the past where you could have
explained misophonia and did not? Why?

_____

_____

_____

_____

Reasonable versus Unreasonable Requests

Perhaps one of the hardest parts of misophonia is deciding which triggers should or should not be accommodated by another person. In practice, this is a constant negotiation. This chart is meant to be filled out together with your partner. If you and your partner cannot agree if a request is reasonable or unreasonable, then this is an area for further negotiations and discussions around that particular trigger.

Reasonable versus Unreasonable Requests Sample

Reasonable Request	Unreasonable Request
• Close your door while playing video games. • Eat chips in another room or with white noise playing. • Have set times to watch movies versus eating.	• Never play video games. • Never eat chips. • Never watch movies since one partner wants to eat throughout.

Reasonable versus Unreasonable Requests Worksheet

Reasonable Request	Unreasonable Request
•	•

Negotiating Boundaries

Unfortunately, there are often triggers that cannot be avoided by the person with misophonia. An example of this is somebody who clears their throat or snores (barring sleep apnea which should get checked out). Some sounds are necessary. More than that, some sounds (and visuals) are part of activities that are important to our partners. This chart is meant to help couples negotiate their "Never", "Sometimes", and "Adapting" triggers. Adapting sounds are ones that are necessary or unavoidable. The adapting portion comes in to help the couple negotiate ways for the misophonia sufferer to live in this environment where triggers are present. The following example is my own chart based on my own triggers, but each couple will have a chart tailored to their situations. These categories can change over time! For example, restaurants used to be in my "Never" category. This list should not be treated like scripture but rather used for couples to identify their needs and boundaries.

Sample Boundary Negotiation Chart

Never	Sometimes	Adapting
• Whistling. • Finger tapping. • Gum chewing. • Leg shaking.	• Popcorn during movies. • Going to restaurants.	• Sneezing. • Coughing. • Chewing. • Sharp S sounds when talking.

Boundary Negotiation Chart

Never	Sometimes	Adapting

Sample Accommodation Letter

To Whom It May Concern,

My name is [Therapist Name] and I have been counselling [Client Name] for the past few months regarding a condition called misophonia, as well as for generalized anxiety and depression. While there is no official diagnosis for misophonia (nor could I diagnose as a counsellor even if there were), there is reliable and valid self-assessment from Duke University which I conducted via telehealth therapy with [Client Name]. On the Duke Misophonia Questionnaire, [Client Name] scored in the [range here] misophonia range, which indicates that symptoms of misophonia are causing a great deal of distress for [Client Name].

I am asking the receiver of this letter if you would consider accommodations for [Client Name] including:

- The ability to take their meals out and not be present in the lunchroom.
- A quiet place to wait or the ability to have another pickup location for their meal.

I am available if you require further explanation regarding these accommodations.

Thank you for your consideration.

Sincerely,

Therapist Name

Activity Decision Flowchart

Some activities are important to our partners, and thus we should make an effort to take their interests, hobbies, and passions into account. Unfortunately, there are some activities which might not be possible for an individual with misophonia. Whether this activity can be substituted for another, done with modifications, or the partner can do the activity on their own or with a friend is entirely up to the couple. This flowchart aims to help you with these decisions. In the case that an alternative activity is chosen, the individual who is giving up their activity should be given first choice of a new more misophonia-friendly activity.

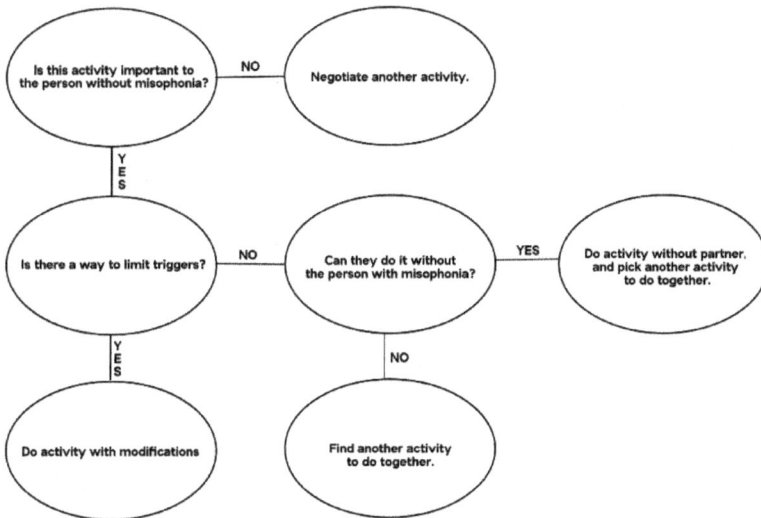

Is this activity important to the person without misophonia? — NO → Negotiate another activity.

YES ↓

Is there a way to limit triggers? — NO → Can they do it without the person with misophonia? — YES → Do activity without partner, and pick another activity to do together.

YES ↓ (Is there a way to limit triggers?)

Do activity with modifications

NO ↓ (Can they do it without the person with misophonia?)

Find another activity to do together.

145

Part 4: Sensory-Based Strategies

Calming the Nervous System

There are numerous ways to calm your nervous system, many of which involve breathing techniques, going into nature, soothing scents, and practicing yoga and meditation. However, there are also strategic sensory tools that can be incorporated. Occupational therapists use what is called a "Sensory Diet" to help with sensory regulation. The degree that these coping skills work for misophonia depends on the person utilizing them. The problem with calming the misophonic nervous system is that if you are still in the room with your trigger, each time you hear the sound you will be re-engaging the fight-flight process.

While this book will offer suggestions for calming the nervous system, it is offered with a caveat: if something does not work for you, or is not enough for the misophonic moment, this is not a failure. It is just an unfortunate part of misophonia that our nervous systems do not habituate to sounds (or visuals), and thus we do not *get used to them*. Because of this, the quickest easiest way to calm the nervous system is to remove the trigger.

With that in mind, I would suggest finding ways to accommodate misophonia that involve leaving the room, learning to ask people not to trigger you, utilizing devices like noise-cancelling headphones/earplugs, and negotiating accommodations in places that you cannot leave. For some therapists, this can seem counterintuitive as the initial response to *fear* in psychology is usually followed by the idea that you should *never feed the monster* and so you should learn to live in those moments. This, however, is a skill traditionally utilized for PTSD, OCD, and anxiety, rather than misophonia, which seems to have neurophysiological and not psychological underpinnings.

People with misophonia are exposed to their triggers daily—whether that is chewing, whistling, tapping, sneezing, or pen clicking. The sounds that cause a misophonic reaction are everywhere, and they are unavoidable. This is not a phobia where a specific stimulus can be avoided at length. For people with misophonia, the next trigger is always creeping around a corner. If exposure cured misophonia, we would all be misophonia-free!

Learning Your Tolerance Level

While there is no amount of *being triggered by misophonia* that is pleasant, most of us with the disorder have a level of stress and anxiety that we can handle before we go from fight-flight-freeze to a complete and utter sensory shutdown. Once we hit this level of tolerance, it can be difficult to bounce back, and some might even experience physical pain or flu-like symptoms. It is important to note that misophonia is worse when your overall stress and anxiety are bad. For example, when you are dealing with the loss of a loved one, school exams, or a work deadline, you are more likely to be triggered because you are not starting out at a baseline calm, but rather are already in a heightened state of arousal before there is even a trigger!

For myself, I have identified which levels of stress I can tolerate and when I absolutely need to leave the environment. I use my Samsung smartwatch to track my overall heart rate and monitor my stress levels. While this is not an overly scientific measure, it is accurate enough to give insightful data on our fight-flight-freeze system. You can also use an Apple smartwatch, a Google smartwatch, a Fitbit device, or even a device from CVS or Amazon costing around $20 that will monitor your heart rate. Using a device to monitor your heart rate is useful as it does not rely on reported feelings which can be hard to parse in the moment. Some people freeze and feel numb, while others feel physical sensations. The use of a heart rate monitor removes this variability by simply relying on data over time. Most of these devices have apps that show historical data.

In my own case, my resting heart rate is roughly 76 to 80. As I become stressed and anxious, this rises to 90-100. While this level is uncomfortable, I am still able to function at a mostly tolerable level. Personally, I have identified a heart rate of 110-120 as my *breaking point* where I need to leave the room or situation immediately. Your own breaking point will be something you will have to determine by cross-referencing your distress to your heart rate and comparing data over time.

Monitoring Your Heart Rate

Monitor your heart rate once per day for one week while you are in a neutral calm state.

1.
2.
3.
4.
5.
6.
7.

Monitor your heart rate once per day for one week while you are in an anxious state, but you are still able to stay in the room.

1.
2.
3.
4.
5.
6.
7.

Monitor your heart rate while you are triggered and experiencing distress. Since this is hopefully less common and variable, simply do so when it happens and not at a set interval.

_____

_____

Compare the results to assess your baseline state, anxious state, and maximum tolerance level.

Baseline:

Anxious:

Maximum Tolerance:

The Sensory Diet

Sensory Diet for Teenagers and Adults

By Susan Nesbit, M.S., OT.

Patricia and Julia Wilbarger coined the term *sensory diet*. Persons with sensory over-responsivity (SOR)—a subtype of sensory processing disorder (SPD)—use sensory diets to stay calm, energized, and organized. Sensory diets are used for SOR in many sensory channels, including the auditory (sounds), the visual (sights), the tactile (touch), and the olfactory (smells). The term SPD often is used interchangeably with SOR, including *auditory over-responsivity*. To be in sync with others, I use the term SPD in this document, unless the narrower term of SOR or auditory-responsivity is needed for clarity.

Whether a sensory diet is also helpful for persons with misophonia is unclear. Sensory diets were developed to treat SOR. If the causes of misophonia are different, then a sensory diet may not be effective. Scholars have speculated that both conditions are neurologically based, and perhaps the same structures in the brain are involved. Scholars have additionally proposed that the limbic system plays a role. The limbic system controls our emotions and the fight-flight-freeze response. The amygdala filters out unimportant and irrelevant sensory information so that it does not reach the limbic system. Deep pressure and slow movement are theorized to help the amygdala act as a filter. If the amygdala plays a role in misophonia, then a sensory diet could lessen the impact of the triggers so that people can respond with less adversity to noxious sounds (triggers). Research is needed to investigate the similarities and the differences between auditory over-responsivity and misophonia.

The purpose of a Sensory Diet is to use a strategic mix of sensory activities to reduce *meltdowns* (e.g., yelling or snapping at someone) and *shutdowns* (withdrawing). Similar to eating food every few hours, the body must be replenished with sensory input. You may need to do a sensory diet every one to two hours. Sensory diets can be used at specific daily time periods or as needed. Choose one or more activities. Doing a sensory diet for 5-15 minutes can be helpful; however, doing a sensory diet for 30 minutes has a longer-lasting effect.

Proprioceptive (pressure) and vestibular (movement) inputs can be calming and organizing. Swinging is the ideal source of *vestibular* input. The effect in the brain from 15 minutes of swinging is reported to last up to eight hours. Other types of sensory input affect the brain for one to two hours. Some experts recommend swinging for at least 15 minutes, two times per day (e.g., early morning and late afternoon). Because a swing hung from one hook can be moved at varying speeds (e.g., fast) and in more directions, using a swing hung from a single hook gives more intense and longer-lasting input than a swing hung from two hooks. Important points: slow, linear, and rhythmical movements are calming, and fast, rotary, and erratic movements are excitatory.

Proprioceptive input is speculated to help integrate vestibular input. Climb and jump after swinging. Proprioceptive input can be used alone without vestibular input. Proprioceptive input is obtained through "heavy work" such as carrying books, moving furniture, vacuuming, and lifting free weights. Proprioceptive input can be calming, energizing, and organizing, so when in doubt, use heavy work (proprioception).

Notes on Other Types of Sensory Input

Auditory (sounds): Many persons with auditory over-responsivity or misophonia can avoid becoming overwhelmed by controlling and predicting the noxious sounds (triggers), so take some control over environmental noises whenever possible.

Visual (sights): Visual input can be over-arousing for persons with auditory sensitivities. Simplify your visual field for a calming and organizing effect. Avoid clothes, towels, rugs, wall colors, etc., in colors that you find distressing. In contrast, if you feel "tuned out", add brightly colored objects to encourage visual attention.

Tactile (touch): Tactile input can be over-arousing. Light touch can be noxious; firm touch can be calming. Avoid clothes with labels, etc., that you find distressing.

Olfactory (smells): Odors calm, stimulate, or send a person into sensory overload. Persons with olfactory over-responsivity can become upset by something "stinky."

Precautions
Avoid using lavender products with boys who have not yet reached puberty. In several recent studies, researchers found a link with breast growth. Experts also suggest not using these products with girls because the effects are not yet known. Lavender also has precautions for adults. When applied to the skin, for example, it sometimes causes irritation.

Other oils can cause irritation when applied directly to the skin. Experiment on small patches of skin before applying oils in large quantities. Putting a few drops into a warm bath can lower the risk of skin irritation. You can use a diffuser to dispense the oils; however, this method has a less intense impact.

Women who are pregnant or breastfeeding should avoid some of the oils listed below. Some of them should be discontinued two weeks prior to surgery, as they can negatively interact with the anesthesia. If you have pets in the home, please be mindful of what essential oils you diffuse as some are poisonous to animals. You should also never diffuse in a room from which a pet cannot escape.

Choosing your scents
Explore the scents to find the ones that best meet your needs, whether this is calming or alerting, and to find the aromas that you prefer. Scents that generally are calming and relaxing are lavender, rose, rosemary, chamomile, ylang-ylang, vanilla, and frankincense. Scents that generally are alerting without causing over-stimulation include citrus extracts which are the best oils for feeling awake (e.g., bergamot, grapefruit, orange, lemon, and

lime), mint (e.g., peppermint and spearmint), pine (e.g., juniper and white fur), eucalyptus, and some herbs and spices (e.g., basil, rosemary, and cinnamon).

Guidelines

For people with SPD, the activities listed in this sensory diet are suggestions. The ideas are not intended to be cookbook recipes. Consider buying the book for the Alert Program to identify your level of arousal and the activities that are calming, energizing, and organizing for you. Alternatively, consult with an occupational therapist for a thorough evaluation and an individualized sensory diet. Use activities based on your interests. Start with something simple and gradually move on to something more challenging. Routines can be important. However, occasionally changing the routine might help you expand your interests if you desire to do so.

Pay attention to your mind/body. Notice when you need to cool off or calm down. Watch for signs that you are starting to relax after switching to calming activities. Activities that work for you one day may not work for you on a different day. Although a sensory diet has consistencies, variations occur from day to day and moment to moment, based on the noxious stimuli that have accumulated on that day at that moment.

Although I listed a particular activity once, putting it into only one category—calming, energizing, or organizing—some of the activities can be used in more than one category. Heavy work (defined as pushing and pulling against resistance and carrying heavy items) can be calming, energizing, and/or organizing. Use a strategic mix of sensory activities by paying attention to your mind/body. When in doubt, use heavy work (proprioception).

Borrowing the wisdom from the quote, "If you know one person with autism, then you know one person with autism", one can say, "If you know one person with SPD, then you know one person with SPD." In other words, all persons with SPD are unique individuals. As a result, the sensory diet that works for one person might not work for another person. Talk with an occupational therapist regularly, when possible, to be certain the sensory diet continues to fit your sensory needs.

Sensory diets should include calming, energizing (alerting), and organizing activities to be used based on your performance. Develop an individualized sensory diet using the lists below as a guide. Use calming activities during periods of high arousal or stress and energizing activities during periods of low arousal or calm.

Calming Activities

If you are over-stimulated, the following activities may help to calm you.

- Hugging/bear hugging with a partner.

- Tightly wrapping your arms around your torso and/or crossing your legs and/or squeezing your hands together.

- Cuddling with a partner or pets.

- Getting a firm massage or backrub with deep/firm pressure—light touch or stroking could be alerting.

- Pushing against a wall with back, buttocks, hands, head, or shoulders.

- Pushing against a wall as if to move it.

- Leaning forward with hands on edge of desk or table— gently pushing as if to move it; doing pushups if table is stable.

- Pushing into a chair with hands on the sides; holding self above chair with both arms; doing chair pushups.

- Rolling up tightly in a blanket.

- Slow rocking in a sleeping bag.

- Slow rocking, e.g., in a rocking chair.

- Swinging with slow, linear, and rhythmical movements (e.g., on a hammock).

- Carrying books or other heavy objects across a room or up and down the stairs.

- Wearing a heavy backpack (precautions: the cautious estimate to prevent injuries is to carry no more than

10% of your body weight, with 15-20% being less cautious estimates; use a backpack with wide and padded shoulder straps, a padded back, and a waist strap; distribute the load so it does not become bottom-heavy or top-heavy, and wear the backpack across both shoulders).

- Wearing a heavy backpack while carrying a few books.

- Wearing weighted collars, pillows, or blankets (heed precautions, especially with weighted vests).

- Taking a slow walk at sunset.

- Walking/strolling in a park.

- Swimming laps.

- Lifting free weights.

- Carrying a laundry basket.

- Washing windows, mirrors, or tables.

- Pushing and pulling heavy items (e.g., yard work)— mowing the lawn (with a push lawn mower), raking, shoveling dirt or snow (heed safety precautions to avoid straining), and pushing firewood in a wheelbarrow.

- Enjoying leisure activities (e.g., reading or listening to books on tape) in a quiet space filled with pillows for cuddling (avoid over-stimulating visual distractions— use dim lighting, close the drapes/shades or sit with your back to the windows, use solid-colored furniture and rugs versus patterned ones and solid-colored walls in soft or neutral colors versus patterned wallpaper in bold colors, hide clutter in bins or boxes or behind doors or curtains—e.g., hang a solid-color curtain over a bookshelf, avoid wearing clothing in colors that you find distressing, and consider asking your loved ones, friends, and colleagues to avoid wearing clothes in colors that you find distressing).

- Watching fish swimming in an aquarium.

- Watching and listening to flames in a bonfire or fireplace, especially a fireplace with real wood.

- Listening to rain, waterfalls, and ocean waves.

- Listening to a tabletop fountain or an aquarium.

- Listening to quiet/soothing/relaxing classical music such as Mozart, Bach, Handel, Pachelbel, and Vivaldi.

- Listening to colored noise (e.g., white, pink, and grey); however, some persons find colored noise to be irritating.

- Taking a warm bath or shower before rolling up in a large towel (avoid using towels in colors that you find distressing).

- Using calming scents such as lavender and/or rose in oils, soaps, lotions, or candles (strong scents can be alerting rather than calming, so experiment).

- Wearing compression clothing, e.g., short-sleeved and long-sleeved t-shirts, shorts, and pants.

Energizing Activities

If you need to be aroused, wake up your senses by trying some of these activities:

- Tug-of-War (pull on a TheraBand tied around the doorknob of a closed door; use the strongest re-sistance possible).

- Pulling heavy items, e.g., suitcase or backpack on wheels.
- Jumping jacks/star jumps on the floor.
- Jumping on a mini trampoline (use a backyard trampoline if one is available).
- Jumping rope.
- Bouncing on a hopper ball, exercise ball, or therapy ball (these balls come in adult sizes).
- Brisk/vigorous walking and race walking.
- Hiking uphill.
- Stair climbing—race up the stairs, then go up the stairs two at a time (to cool off, walk at a normal pace down the stairs).
- Aerobics, including chair aerobics.
- Calisthenics, e.g., lunges, squat jumps, situps, pushups, and pullups.
- Tumbling, e.g., cartwheels.
- Swimming—doing flips and somersaults in the water.
- Swing dancing.
- Spinning in rotating chair or on swing suspended from one hook.
- Using playground swings or a merry-go-round (you are never too old!).
- Taking a cool shower.
- Using alerting scents such as citrus, mint, and/or pine in oils, soaps, lotions, or candles.

Organizing Activities

These activities may calm or energize, depending on your needs. Pay attention to your body for signs that indicate your level of arousal.

- Squeezing stress balls.
- Sucking, e.g., water from a squeeze bottle, a popsicle, or a lifesaver.
- Sucking drinkable (liquid) yogurt through a straw.
- Eating healthy crunchy foods like carrots or chewy foods like jellybeans.
- Chewing bubblegum.
- Blowing soap bubbles.
- Climbing stairs (up and down) or a ladder.
- Doing pushups (on the floor from knees or toes; standing and leaning forward against a wall).
- Doing situps.
- Doing jumping jacks.
- Tumbling and gymnastics.
- Doing headstands or handstands against a wall.
- Hiking, walking, or running.
- Roller skating, roller blading, or ice skating.
- Jumping rope.
- Biking/cycling.
- Horseback riding.
- Stretching, including tai chi and yoga.
- Lying on your stomach to read a book.
- Painting the walls with plain and/or textured paints, e.g., add sand to the paint.
- Pushing heavy items, e.g., shopping cart, laundry basket, or box filled with books.

- Pulling heavy items, e.g., wagon filled with children, books, or laundry detergent.
- Vacuuming—especially when pushing the furniture out of the way!
- Taking out the rubbish/garbage/trash or hauling bags of leaves to the curb.
- Creating a scrapbook—ripping/tearing paper, using different textures, gluing (squeeze bottle) or pasting, and painting.
- Coloring mandalas—begin at the center and work your way to the outside border; use colored pencils or crayons because markers leak and destroy the experience.
- Sewing, knitting, crocheting, and weaving.
- Sculpting—making things out of clay through coil or slab methods; try using a potter's wheel.
- Woodworking—sawing, gluing in dowels, pounding nails, screwing in nuts and bolts, using sandpaper to smooth the project.
- Baking—mixing the ingredients in a bowl (not using an electric mixer) and squeezing/kneading, flattening, and rolling the dough for bread or cookies.
- Cooking—pounding chicken cutlets with a food hammer and chopping vegetables.
- Gardening—digging, patting soil, pulling weeds, carrying and pouring water from a large watering can, and pouring/dumping dirt or mulch.

Organizing Games and Partnership or Group Activities

- Tug-of-War.

- Tennis or badminton.

- Softball or baseball.

- Volleyball.

- Basketball.

- Kickball or soccer.

- Martial arts, including taekwondo and karate.

- Races, e.g., adult relay races, 5K and 10K runs, half and full marathons, and track and field.

- Dancing and singing.

Example of a Sensory Diet

Personalize this example. To meet your changing sensory needs, modify the activities as your needs change. Use a strategic mix of activities.

General suggestions: Take frequent movement breaks, sit on an inflatable wobble cushion, and chew crunchy foods (e.g., carrots) during daily activities that require attention and concentration. Rocking gently before bedtime can help with a sleeping problem. Try a firm self-hug after rocking.

In the morning:

- Upon awakening, massage your neck and shoulders—gently but firmly move your fingers in small circles—start at the base of your skull and move down your neck and then out toward one shoulder and repeat toward the other shoulder—work out the knots—then stretch by hugging yourself.
- Take a bath or a cool shower with alerting scents such as citrus, mint, or pine.
- Use a vibrating toothbrush and/or a vibrating hairbrush.
- Listen to music that you find alerting but not over-stimulating.
- Eat crunchy cereal with fruit and some protein.
- Take a brisk or vigorous walk or jump on a mini trampoline.

Midafternoon:

- Do aerobic exercises or jump on a mini trampoline.
- Go for a bicycle ride or do yoga.
- Push a grocery cart or a stroller, depending on family needs.
- Massage your feet to "reorganize".
- Listen to music that you find alerting but not over-stimulating.
- Oral work—suck liquid yogurt through a straw, eat crunchy and chewy snacks, or chew gum before and/or during activities at a desk or table.

At dinnertime:

- Make a meal involving mixing, chopping, pounding, and so on.
- Set the table using two hands to carry and balance a heavy but stable tray.
- Eat crunchy and chewy foods.

At night:

- Take a walk/stroll in a park.
- Sew, sculpt clay, or make woodworking projects or scrapbooks.
- Color mandalas—begin at the center and work your way to the outside border; use colored pencils or crayons.
- Take a warm bath with bubbles and calming essential oils such as lavender or rose.

- Give yourself a massage.
- Listen to quiet/soothing/relaxing classical music such as Mozart, Bach, Handel, Pachelbel, and Vivaldi.

Create Your Own Sensory Diet

In the morning:

_____
_____
_____
_____
_____

Midafternoon:

_____
_____
_____
_____

At dinnertime:

_____
_____
_____
_____

At night:

_____
_____
_____
_____
_____

Coping When Busy or Overwhelmed

Sometimes coping with misophonia is easier said than done. You or your client might understand that a sensory diet or cognitive skills can be helpful, and yet struggle to implement these strategies in everyday life. When the body is overwhelmed and dysregulated, it can be hard to implement strategies to help. It is important for people with misophonia to realize that this is not a failure of moral strength or willpower. In his book *Self-Reg*, Dr. Stuart Shanker explains that "It is by being regulated that a child develops the ability to self-regulate" (Shanker and Barker, 2016). Although this sentiment is speaking about children, dysregulated children who are not given adequate coping skills grow up to be dysregulated adults.

Coping skills are something that must be developed and practiced, and they are also something that can be hard to implement in day-to-day life when we are already struggling to get by. The idea of coping and self-regulation can sound like another thing to add to a never-ending to-do list. For people who are overwhelmed by the idea of utilizing coping skills, it can be helpful to incorporate passive activities which help regulate without being taxing and hard to keep up with. For example, a scent diffuser can help calm the nervous system and be used in a set-and-forget manner.

Here are some suggestions for ways to cope that do not require people to go out of their way to incorporate coping skills into their day-to-day lives:

- Diffusers with essential oils that you find calming.
- Shower steamers which are like bath bombs but can be used in the shower with calming scents.
- A weighted blanket to sleep in at night.
- Incorporating small amounts of exercise such as walking stairs instead of using elevators.
- Choosing activities that calm you instead of agitate you; for example, watching a comedy show instead of a horror movie when upset.

The idea is that as you build your own sensory diet and coping skills, you ensure they are realistic for the life that you are living. Your coping skills should not add more stress and discomfort to your life.

Finding Coping Skills You Can Easily Incorporate

Passive coping skills are coping skills that you can incorporate into your life with little to no additional effort. Active coping skills require a little more planning, so they should be chosen carefully. The goal is to choose activities that fit into your life and that do not overwhelm you.

Passive Coping Skills	Active Coping Skills
Sleeping with a weighted blanket.	Sew, sculpt clay, do woodworking projects, or scrapbook.
Shower or bath steamers/bombs for scent therapy.	Make a meal involving mixing, chopping, pounding, and so on.
An essential oil diffuser in your room.	Carrying books or other heavy objects across a room or up and down the stairs.
Changing your curtains to a light-blocking style.	Swimming laps.
Wearing a heavy weighted vest.	Switching to taking stairs instead of an elevator.
Listening to colored noise (e.g., white, pink, and grey).	Going for regular walks, and even better if they are in a calming nature environment.

Fill out your own passive/active coping skills list.

Passive Coping Skills	Active Coping Skills

Creating a Safe Space

Whether the person with misophonia is a child, a teenager, or an adult, having a safe space in their home to calm down is an integral part of coping with misophonia. Since misophonia involves being dysregulated with a state of panic and fear, safety is an important means of managing this disorder. This safe space can be as small as a closet, or as large as an entire room. This is of course dependent on the space available to the person with misophonia. If there are no spaces in the home available, such as with a roommate in a shared living situation, one potential accommodation is a bed tent. Bed tents are set up over your bed, with your mattress inside, creating a safe and private space without taking up extra room in the home.

As much as reasonably possible, the safe space should be quiet, lit in a way that is amenable to the sufferer, and be generally soothing to the person it is designed for. In an otherwise loud space, a noise generator or fan can be used to drown out sounds. The use of headphones, earplugs, and music can also be helpful to enhance the space.

With the sensory diet in mind, this safe space can be filled with activities, scents, and materials that the person finds calming. For example, within this room we could find painting supplies, a white noise machine, a diffuser for essential oils, teddy bears to hug, and dimmable lights. This experience will be different for each person and will of course vary based on the layout of a home. This sensory space could even be a living room or bedroom if you plan for it accordingly. The idea is to have a set space to calm down when overstimulated.

The following is a non-exhaustive list of things that could be present in a sensory-safe space:

- Sensory toys such as chewable necklaces or fidget toys.
- A scent diffuser or candle.
- Coloring books, art supplies, and other craft supplies.
- Books to read.
- Stuffed animals or comfy pillows to hug.
- Galaxy lamps (these are lamps that turn the ceiling into a starry night).
- A weighted blanket.
- Playdough, kinetic sand, or slime.

The idea of this sensory space is that it is a calming retreat from an otherwise busy and overwhelming world. This does not have to be a formalized space necessarily, but it is about choosing activities and environmental factors that are calming rather than overstimulating. For this reason, I did not suggest using television since this could be overstimulating with both visuals and sounds. However, some people may find classic TV shows, Disney movies, or even horror movies to be calming—and if that is the case, then go for it!

Planning Your Sensory Space

Where is your sensory space?

_____

_____

What items do you already have that you can add to your sensory space?

_____

_____

_____

_____

What changes could you make to your sensory space to make it calmer?

_____

_____

_____

_____

When will you come to your sensory space?

_____

_____

_____

_____

Part 5: Cognitive and Psychological Strategies

Dealing with the Emotions of Misophonia

While the initial trigger for misophonia is in the physical processes of the brain and cannot be controlled, the emotional responses that linger after the triggers are no longer present are something that people with misophonia have some ability to manage. This is not to say that we can eliminate the trigger response and subsequent emotional turmoil, but rather that we can work on cognitive and psychological strategies to ensure that these emotions do not persist longer than necessary. There is some evidence that cognitive behavioral therapy is beneficial for misophonia (Jager et al., 2021), and thus is a meaningful coping skill to include.

The idea is to manage the emotions surrounding misophonia, rather than expecting that we can eliminate the trigger response. For example, a person cannot stop a trigger from causing a fight-flight response, but they can become adaptive to these triggers, learn to self-advocate, or employ sensory or cognitive skills to calm down. The following section includes several worksheets to help change beliefs and perceptions of misophonia and focus on how persons with misophonia can become adaptive rather than reactive. These worksheets can be copied and used more than once or written upon directly in this book. How they are used is up to the individual or the clinician utilizing the worksheets.

Accepting Misophonia

Lately, I have been thinking regularly about grief. Misophonia is a tough condition to live with. It takes over our lives, our relationships, and it isolates us. We often feel as though we have drawn the shortest straw. It can be tough to look at others—perfectly normal and able to sit on a bus without bursting into tears. Each and every day we are faced with triggers and unfortunately they seem to get worse with time and exposure.

I have lost many people in my life, and I have experienced grief in its rawest form. After sitting across from my grandmother, her hand in mine, as she took her last breath, I knew I would have to learn to adjust. Misophonia is not different from this. You have lost something—the chance to live your life free of triggers. Despite your desire to push it away, you must face misophonia.

You cannot repress your emotions. You must find a way to come to terms with it, accept it, and live your life. I understand that this can be one of the most frustrating situations in the world. I have had my fair share of moments where I have dashed off to the restroom and cried as much as I could. I have kicked a brick wall in an attempt to quell the rage. I have left classes, family dinners, and other important situations to go home to my bed and stay there. I have avoided my life for days and at my worst for weeks. I admit that I have depression that makes misophonia worse. However, I would have gladly lived most of my days in a state of depression rather than with the triggers of misophonia.

Sometimes I still feel this way, but it is not as often. The reason is that I now understand that like any chronic illness, any friend who slips through the cracks, and any life-altering unchangeable event out of our control, misophonia causes grief.

I firmly believe that in order to live a fulfilling life, we need to understand that there is currently no cure. We should know that our lives and their meaningfulness is not measured by the number of days without triggers. This disorder may have a hold, but it is not our life. We are important and we need to understand that this grief should go through the same stages as any other loss.

Denial and Isolation

Denial can come in different ways. People with misophonia may at first believe that they are just "hyper-sensitive" or that it is their fault. It is also no secret that misophonia often leads to self-inflicted isolation.

Anger

It makes sense to be angry with misophonia. It is a life-changing existence-altering condition, not to mention the rage that is associated with the trigger itself.

Bargaining

Sufferers may try to find help in ways that have a small chance of working. This can involve using therapies that have either not been tested or approved.

Depression

Since misophonia is an isolating condition, it is not surprising that sufferers have increased sadness and feelings of hopelessness.

Acceptance

You must come to terms with your disorder. It will be okay.

Accepting that you have misophonia does not mean that you have given up on anything. It is quite the opposite. Instead of spending your time thinking of everything that you have lost and what you cannot do, you should be exploring opportunities to enjoy your life. Living with a disorder does not mean sacrifice, but rather it means adjustments. For example, you could do a degree online if you cannot handle regular school. Perhaps if you are unable to fly, you could drive or take a cruise. The key is to find ways to adapt to the life you have, not the life you wish you had.

Misophonia Checklist: Be Proactive

Remember, paying attention to your physiological state before the misophonic moment can help you cope!

	Complete a sensory-based calming activity before entering the moment (such as yoga, stretching, use of a weighted blanket).
	Earplugs (if you use them).
	Headphones with white noise or sound generators.
	Items you or your child find calming for the misophonic moment.
	Reassurance that even if things do not go "perfectly" that it is going to be okay!

Create your own checklist based on your needs. You can write this on a piece of paper or create an image and put it on your wall.

Thinking About Coping

How did you cope the last time you were triggered?

_____

_____

_____

_____

Do you think there is something you could have done differently?

_____

_____

_____

_____

What is something you could use from the Sensory Diet to help you cope the next time you are triggered?

_____

_____

_____

_____

Misophonia Reflection

What happened...

_____

_____

_____

_____

_____

How I feel about it...

_____

_____

_____

_____

_____

What could be different next time?

_____

_____

_____

_____

_____

Thinking About Triggers

When did you first notice your misophonia?

_____

_____

When is the last time you remember having a new trigger?

_____

_____

Name a time when you were triggered and handled it well.

_____

_____

Name a time when you were triggered and did not handle it well.

_____

_____

What was the difference between when you handled your trigger well and when you did not handle your trigger well?

_____

_____

Reframing Misophonia

Reframing is a cognitive tool that is used to help cope with negative emotions. Although the trigger for misophonia happens before we have an emotional response, we can still reframe our beliefs about misophonia. The idea here is to write down our negative thoughts about misophonia and then re-write them in a way that no longer associates the origin of the trigger as the instigator.

Example
Misophonia thought: Why did he have to whistle? It is so rude. I hate whistling. This is so cruel.

Misophonia thought re-framed: He probably does not know whistling upsets me. Maybe he is happy or trying to keep himself calm.

Misophonia thought:

_____

_____

Misophonia thought re-framed:

_____

_____

Examining the Misophonic Moment

What is the trigger?

_____

_____

Who or what is the trigger emanating from?

_____

_____

Why is the trigger sound/visual being made?

_____

_____

Is there anything adaptive you can do to stop it?

_____

_____

How can you adapt to the trigger if it cannot be stopped?

_____

_____

The Empty Chair

The Empty Chair is a form of Gestalt therapy where the person who is trying to overcome their emotions sits opposite an empty chair and expresses how they feel to the chair. For persons with misophonia, this could be used by either the sufferer of misophonia or by the person who is often causing the triggering sound.

Instructions

- Place an empty chair across from where you are going to sit during this exercise.
- Spend 10 to 20 minutes explaining how you feel to the empty chair. It is best to think of one common theme (such as your chewing popcorn during movies upsets me).
- Take some time to reflect and allow this to sink in. Were you surprised by your feelings?
- Switch your position into the other chair. You are now taking on the role of your partner. For 10 to 20 minutes, consider how they feel and express what you think they are feeling. Perhaps the response is "Not being able to enjoy a snack during a movie feels like I am missing out on the experience I am used to."
- Reflect on your roleplay as your partner. How did that feel?

This exercise could be used by either partner in the relationship.

Write Your Article

Writing articles about misophonia can be a very therapeutic process. By writing an article about misophonia, you are able to process your stressors and tell your story. Whether you write this article to publish or simply for your own journal, this process is one of exploration of your disorder. If you like, this article can even be published on your own blog or submitted to Misophonia International. This is entirely optional, but always available to members of the misophonia community to share our stories and learn from one another.

Things you could include in your article.

- How misophonia impacts you.
- How you cope with misophonia.
- What people without misophonia should know.
- What would you tell somebody who just learned about misophonia?
- Tell a particular story about misophonia (for example, living with misophonia when sick; living with misophonia at college).

The point of the article is to reflect on your point of view regarding misophonia while refocusing from a more neutral standpoint. Consider the audience as you write, rather than yourself.

Example Article

This example article was one that I personally used for coping with misophonia half a decade ago.

The Life of a Young Adult with Misophonia

Like a ghost, the memory of finger-tapping has become my own personal poltergeist. I feel jolted just as one would if the doors were slamming—if the lights were erratically going on and off.

I lie in bed and I replay each finger tap. I do not want to think about it—but like bullets from a gun I replay every second. Bump. Bump. The ferocity echoes through my brain—the noise, god the noise—it is just as loud as it was in person.

At twenty-four years old, I should be living every moment of my life to the fullest. I should be partying, making mistakes, and spending long wistful nights walking barefoot in the park. I should be kissing strangers in alleyways, because I am young and mistakes are part of what makes life worth living. I should be drinking a little too much and stumbling home just before the sun rises. I have a desire to do these things. I want to be young and careless. I want to go out for the night without prior planning, and I want to live my life to the fullest. Instead, I am trapped. I am locked into a world that is dictated by a disorder that suffocates my lust for life. Every decision is marred by its touch. I have gone to clubs, and I have had some fun, but I am increasingly losing my ability to be young and carefree. Instead, I am young and restless.

I have misophonia. While the internet is busy classifying us as a strange, weird, or violent disorder, the truth is a little more depressing. It is true that many of us are upset by chewing—but this disorder goes much further than frustration when our family members crunch down on potato chips. Many of us often struggle from sensory problems similar to that of Sensory Processing Disorder. This disorder is more than an aversion to sounds—it is an all-encompassing prison.

The strangest part is that when there are no sounds, I am normal. It is as though the disorder has evaporated. I am still myself. I will be going about my life like everybody else. I walk like a person that has never been troubled. Everything is fine. Until it is not.

Imagine for a second that you are trapped in a cave with a dripping faucet. This faucet would continue and eventually become torture. For those of us with misophonia, we are immediately trapped in the cave. Because of our amygdala, we do not get used to sounds. Instead, we are bombarded by a fight-flight response. We are constantly sick, anxious, and living in a world where our bodies are sensorily taxed. Much deeper than simple anger, we are often isolated from our lives. There is no cure for misophonia, and increased exposure can make the disorder worse. Because of this, and the cycle of pain and anxiety, we are more likely to avoid unnecessary social events. Further than that, if I were to "push myself", I am likely to end up with a severe migraine.

The normal life of a twenty-four-year-old is something I am not going to have. It has taken some time to adjust to the idea that, unless the research of the Misophonia and Emotion Regulation Program of Duke is successful, I may be living with this severe condition for much of my adult life. Truth be told, I am terrified. The life of a young adult with misophonia is a confusing one. I have not been out, or partied, in over a year. Since social groups are often how we define our youth—I have had to find interests that are solitary. I have not been on a date in a year either. As the disorder worsens, my interests have been chipped away one by one—the memory of events, and the risk of them repeating, has been the deciding factor in many of my activities.

If I were to go on a date, it would have to be something small and solitary. Movie theatres, due to the popcorn, leg-shaking, and loud noises, are simply impossible. Restaurants also have chewing, and I generally avoid any situation where people are sitting down. Sitting in a car can be hard if the person rests their arm on the windowsill or taps their fingers on the car wheel. I cannot control my fight-flight reaction, and it is hard to explain to others why it is happening when there are little resources and awareness to point them to—I am exasperated as I try to explain that it is not them I am mad at, but the sound itself is causing my brain to go into overdrive and short circuit. Sadly, it has become easier to not explain at all. To simply stay home and control what is going to happen.

A day for me usually begins with the night. During normal daytime hours there are honking horns, lawnmowers, buzzing motors, screaming children, and persons that inevitably may show up at the door. Instead, I have opted for a life that takes place during the hours of 8PM and 10AM. There are still noises, even in this sheltered life. Even in a world that is considered rural compared to cities. No days are without triggers, and as these triggers mount, I become sick. After triggers, my muscles tense so tight that I have back pain, I become nauseated and dizzy. If I do not remove myself from the situation, these symptoms become worse. The longest migraine from misophonia that I have had was 7 days long. When dealing with reactions this strong, avoidance becomes the main tool in your arsenal.

The world of misophonia and over-responsivity means that some clothes are too tight, lights are far too bright, and we are more likely to get migraines. Scent allergies are common, and perfume can quickly make us sick. Visuals can cause the fight-flight response too. Effectively, we are being threatened by everyday occurrences at a level that can be hard to explain—we are also attacked by media that is convinced we are overreacting or are a "think-piece". After all, it is strange and unruly to think that the regular world could be causing people so much distress. Unfortunately, I am here to tell you that this condition is very real.

The life of a young adult with misophonia is the life of a girl who was making As and Bs in university her first term—then, as triggers grew, attendance dropped. Eventually, to continue at all, I had to switch to online school. I became so suffocated by the triggers that I could not hear what was going on in the classroom. To even survive the class, I would have to distract myself—and nothing was enough to distract from pen clicking, from legs shaking, and other students that were simply trying to learn. For me, I was trying to survive. Like many other young adult experiences, the college life was another that I had to step back from. While I am still finishing my degree online, it is taking much longer. The social connection and wonderful memories that accompanied my first year have been replaced by my bedroom and textbooks. While I love learning, there is a loss that has taken place.

Misophonia is not chewing rage, sound rage, or "murderous rage". Misophonia is loneliness. It is the loss of social relationships and the decaying of what we could have been, or what we used to be. Misophonia is a daily fight and struggle. We must remain hopeful despite every life change, despite the sickness, and despite being trapped in fight-flight much of our days. Misophonia is resilience, because if we can survive this and still accomplish some of our goals, we have fought the toughest battle of all—the battle against our own brains.

Turning Misophonia into Fiction

Turning misophonia into fiction has been very therapeutic in my own life. In fact, I wrote an entire novel which showcases a character with misophonia. I am not saying that you need to write a novel, nor do you even need to write a cohesive story. The idea is that you take your misophonia and instead of writing from your own perspective, you create a character through which you can process these emotions. You might be surprised where your imagination takes you in your fictitious scenario. The idea is to write without planning and allow your imagination to take you places you were not expecting.

Example fiction (excerpt from How We Survive Ourselves)

Adra

Like a ghost, the memory of the finger-tapping has become my own personal poltergeist. I feel jolted just as one would if the doors were slamming—if the lights were erratically going on and off. They may as well be.

It takes days to recover from each meeting with people. Now that I know Jason may tap his fingers, I do not want to go back. The incident has played over and over in my mind. Without trying, he has occupied every space of my thoughts. Even as he tries to help me, he has become part of the problem.

I lie in bed, and I replay each finger tap. I do not want to think about it, but like bullets from a gun, I replay every second. Bump. Bump. The ferocity echoes through my brain—the noise, god the noise—it is just as loud as it was in person. Even the movement scrapes at the side of my brain.

I dread going back to therapy. I dread being here, but I also do not want to go home. The noises were bad there too. The noises are bad no matter where I go. At first, they were not that bad. They were annoying. Now, as it goes on, they are getting worse. I feel like a computer program that is broken. Or maybe I am not even the software. Maybe I am trying to reinstall Windows on a hard drive that is already cracked and shattered. No matter how many doctors try, this is not going to work. My brain is damaged, and there is no one that can help me.

No one has the answers that can help me. It repeats on loop with each memory.

The strangest part is that when I am normal, and there are no sounds, I am still myself. I am not crazy, but the sounds bring me from myself instantly.

In the time it takes for me to get up, get dressed, and make my way to the cafeteria, nothing has happened. I walk like a person that has never been troubled. I choose my foods, and I choose a spot to eat. Everything is fine.

Until it is not.

I can see them, and they cannot see me. I hear chewing as soon as it happens—a potato chip—and a few girls shake their legs. Turmoil is quick. I feel my brain shake. I have to steady myself. I will not cry. I sit down and attempt to eat. Slow bites that barely make it to my mouth. I force my spoon. I chose soup because it is quick. I did not consider the slurping noises from the soup of the girl next to me. With every "ss" sound, I grow more anxious.

My palms are sweating, and my eyes dart to the exits. I stare at my bowl, and I count how many bites there are left. If I eat fast, I can probably finish it in 10, but that is ten sips too many.

I move my hand over my face and re-arrange my hair. It covers some of the leg shaking, but I still know it is there. I take another mouthful of soup tentatively. I feel compelled to check to see if she is gone. I fight that urge. Not knowing is almost better. Only almost. I feel it dig away at me. I know she is there. I hear the girl with the soup again, and my world becomes a blur. I am tired, and I am angry. I do not know if it is the sound making me mad or the pain that accompanies it. My body feels like it has been moved against a giant cheese grater.

I quickly get up and throw all nine sips of soup in the garbage on my way to the door. I do not stop in the hallway. I move fast through people sitting before I can tell what their legs are doing. I decide that I do not need to eat anymore. I will figure something out. Maybe I will pay an orderly to hide food in my room. I do not care. I just need out. I think about the soup. I am mad at myself for eating the same thing that tortured me. No, it is not the soup. It is how she was eating it. Her slurping—who slurps like that? She must be a child, I think. I know it is irrational and unfair to her, but my brain is tossing and turning trying to find an explanation.

I am delirious by the time I make it back to my room. Tears are welled in my eyes, and the tension from the experience lives in each of my muscles. I should talk to Jason, but I am too tired. I feel as though I have been held under water. I cannot explain to him right now. I cannot leave my room and see the sights that make me crazy or hear the sounds.

I push my weight against my door, making sure it is closed. I am thankful for the noise-proof rooms. We have emergency buttons in case something happens, but we are allowed silence. For me, I am grateful that in this room, I cannot see or hear the others. This is the second greatest thing to a padded room. It is solitude. Freedom. Silence.

With my clothes still on, I lie back on my bed. Why did I bother leaving my room? The entire world is out to get me, and the sooner I recognize this, the sooner I can just come to terms with my prison.

As I calm down, I realize I may get bored eventually. Boredom is a small price to pay for avoiding the trauma. I try to consider things I could do. If I could find one friend that will not trigger me, then maybe I could be okay. I cannot do that; everybody will trigger me eventually. The noises. The visuals. The people. They are everywhere. Even when it is over, it is never over.

I try to erase the memory from my mind. Nothing seems to work. I hold my breath. I sing a song aloud. Nothing erases the memory of the sounds. Distraction would help, but now my room has become a tiny little box. I do not know what I am supposed to do. I want to reach out and talk to someone. I want someone to understand what is going on in my brain.

When they ask what drove me mad, what drove me to the brink of my brain exploding, the answer is not going to be war or terror. It is going to be soup.

Your Fiction

_____

_____

_____

_____

_____

_____

_____

_____

_____

_____

_____

_____

_____

_____

_____

Reimagining Misophonia

Think of a time when you experienced a distressing situation involving misophonia. Perhaps this was in public, at school, or with a loved one. Instead of recreating this event, re-write the event in a way that you wish it had happened. You could include sensory-based strategies, psychoeducation (teaching the person about misophonia), or negotiating accommodations. How you re-write the scenario is up to you.

Your Reimagined Scenario

_____

_____

_____

_____

_____

_____

_____

_____

_____

_____

_____

_____

The Miracle Question

If you woke up tomorrow and you no longer had misophonia, how would you react? What would you do?

_____

_____

_____

_____

_____

_____

_____

_____

_____

_____

_____

_____

_____

_____

_____

_____

_____

_____

_____

Choosing a Mantra

Some people with misophonia find choosing a mantra for the misophonic moment to be helpful. The purpose of your mantra should be to both distract yourself from the trigger and remind yourself that you are technically *safe*.

For example: "I am safe. This is not forever. I will be okay."

"It is the sound/visual causing this. I will be okay when it is over."

Write your own mantra

_____

_____

_____

_____

What if You Feel Guilty or Bitter that You Need Accommodations?

Some people with misophonia have expressed to me that they feel uncomfortable always using assistive technology or accommodations for misophonia. I think it is important to consider these thoughts of *guilt* or *shame* that we might feel by using these technologies such as earplugs, sensory tools, earphones, or noise generators. Perhaps as a child you were told that your misophonia was a "you problem" and you internalized that you should "just get over it", or maybe you worry that others seeing you wearing these devices will judge you and think there is something wrong with you. It is natural to worry about the way those in our environment feel about us, and perhaps ironically, this is also part of threat detection. The outsider of a group has less safety as they do not have the protection of the collective.

When it comes to accommodating misophonia, I personally believe that sufferers should feel empowered to use the tools that help them mitigate the disorder. For example, we would not accost a person who is deaf for using hearing aids, and we would never berate a person in need of a wheelchair. While misophonia is not yet as accepted by the wider public, I think sufferers should at the very least show the same grace to themselves as they would to a stranger or a loved one suffering with a more "accepted" condition.

Misophonia is a lifelong struggle and thus it is a marathon and not a sprint. The tools that we learn to adopt for misophonia should be utilized as needed, without shame. It is my hope that the sufferers of misophonia and clinicians reading this book see accommodation and advocacy as the cornerstone to managing and mitigating misophonia.

Conclusion

Coping with misophonia is not a linear process. Instead, coping is an everyday moment-to-moment endeavor that involves self-advocacy, accommodations, and utilizing sensory and cognitive/psychological skills to manage the condition. Rather than reading this book once and setting it aside, I suggest if possible that you bookmark the parts that feel helpful and come back to them as needed.

As a final reminder to both persons with misophonia and clinicians, I want to reiterate that coping with misophonia is not a "one-size-fits-all" approach, and the degree to which these coping skills work can vary person to person and moment to moment. To leave on a final note, I have the following advice: Do the best you can, and do not feel guilty if some days are better than others.

The Misophonia Matters Class

The *Misophonia Matters* classes are held through The International Misophonia Foundation and are largely based on this book. These classes include the sections featured in this book as well as a questions and answers portion.

You can sign up for a class at www.misophoniafoundation.com/classes.

If you have purchased this book in print or ebook from a vendor other than The International Misophonia Foundation you may obtain a digital DRM-free copy (epub, mobi, and PDF) free of charge for your personal use, or use with clients.

https://misophoniafoundation.com/shop/misophonia-matters-ebook-drm-free/

Use coupon code "MBSFAJQ5" without the quotations to get the ebook 100% free.

References

Ayres, A. J. (1968). Sensory integrative processes and neuropsychological learning disability. *Learning Disorders,* 3.

Ayres, A. J. (1972). *Sensory integration and learning disorders.* Los Angeles: Western Psychological Services.

Ayres, A. J. (1979). *Sensory integration and the child.* Los Angeles: Western Psychological Services.

The Bowen Center for the Study of the Family. (n.d.). https://www.thebowencenter.org/

Brout, J.J., Edelstein, M., Erfanian, M., Mannino, M., Miller, L.J., Rouw, R., Kumar, S., & Rosenthal, M.Z. (2018). Investigating misophonia: A review of the empirical literature, clinical implications, and a research agenda. *Frontiers in Neuroscience*, 12(36).

Brout, J.J. (2021). A clinician's guide to understanding and managing misophonia from a self-regulation perspective: Regulate, reason, reassure. *The International Misophonia Research Network.*

Dunn, W. (2014). Sensory profile 2. Bloomington, MN, USA: Psych Corporation.

Jager, I.J., Vulink, N.C.C., Bergfeld, I.O., van Loon, A.J.J.M., & Denys, D.A.J.P. (2021). Cognitive behavioral therapy for misophonia: A randomized clinical trial. *Depression and Anxiety,* 38(7).

Jastreboff, M. M., & Jastreboff, P. J. (2001). Components of decreased sound tolerance: Hyperacusis, misophonia, phonophobia. *ITHS Newsletter.*

Kumar, S., Tansley-Hancock, O., Sedley, W., Winston, J.S., Callaghan, M.F., Allen, M., Cope, T.E., Gander, P.E., Bamiou, D.E., & Griffiths, T.D. (2017). The brain basis for misophonia. *Current Biology,* 27(4).

Kumar, S., Dheerendra, P., Erfanian, M., Benzaquén, E., Sedley, W., Gander, P.E., Lad, M., Bamiou, D.E., & Griffiths, T.D. (2021). The motor basis for misophonia. *Journal of Neuroscience*, 41(26).

LeBouef, T., Yaker, Z., & Whited, L. (2023). Physiology, autonomic nervous system. *StatPearls Publishing.* https://www.ncbi.nlm.nih.gov/books/NBK538516/

Miller, L.J., Nielsen, D.M., Schoen, S.A., & Brett-Green, B.A. (2009). Perspectives on sensory processing disorder: A call for translational research. *Frontiers in Integrative Neuroscience*, 3(22).

Miller, L.J., Marco, E.J., Chu, R.C., & Camarata, S. (2021). Editorial: sensory processing across the lifespan: A 25-year initiative to understand neurophysiology, behaviors, and treatment effectiveness for sensory processing. *Frontiers in Integrative Neuroscience*, 15.

Moncrieff, J. (2018). Against the stream: Antidepressants are not antidepressants—An alternative approach to drug action and implications for the use of antidepressants. *BJPsych Bulletin,* 42(1).

Nesbit, S. (n.d). The sensory diet for adults and teens. *Misophonia International.*

Piccardi, E. S., & Gliga, T. (2022). Understanding sensory regulation in typical and atypical development: The case of sensory seeking. *Developmental Review*, 65.

Porcaro, C.K., Alavi, E., Gollery, T., & Danesh, A.A. (2019). Misophonia: Awareness and responsiveness among academics. *Journal of Postsecondary Education and Disability,* 32(2).

Rinaldi, L.J., Simner, J., Koursarou, S., & Ward, J. (2023). Autistic traits, emotion regulation, and sensory sensitivities in children and adults with misophonia. *Journal of Autism and Developmental Disorders,* 53(3).

Rosenthal, M.Z., Anand, D., Cassiello-Robbins, C., Williams, Z.J., Guetta, R.E., Trumbull, J., & Kelley, L.D. (2021). Development and initial validation of the duke misophonia questionnaire. *Frontiers in Psychology,* 12.

Rosenthal, M.Z., McMahon, K., Greenleaf, A.S., Cassiello-Robbins, C., Guetta, R., Trumbull, J., Anand, D., Frazer-Abel, E.S., & Kelley, L. (2022). Phenotyping misophonia: Psychiatric disorders and medical health correlates. *Frontiers in Psychology,* 13.

Schröder, A., Vulink, N., & Denys, D. (2013). Misophonia: Diagnostic criteria for a new psychiatric disorder. *PLOS ONE,* 8(1).

Schröder, A., van Wingen, G., Eijsker, N., San Giorgi, R., Vulink, N.C., Turbyne, C., & Denys, D. (2019). Misophonia is associated with altered brain activity in the auditory cortex and salience network. *Scientific Reports,* 9(1).

Shanker, S., & Barker, T. (2016). *Self-Reg: How to help your child (and you) break the stress cycle and successfully engage with life.* Canada: Penguin Random House.

Ungvarsky, J. (2022). Bowenian family therapy. *Salem Press Encyclopedia.*

Waxenbaum, J.A., Reddy, V., & Varacallo, M. (2023). Anatomy, autonomic nervous system. *StatPearls Publishing.* https://www.ncbi.nlm.nih.gov/books/NBK539845/